CAMBRIDGE TEXTS IN THE HISTORY
OF PHILOSOPHY

KIERKEGAARD
Fear and Trembling

CAMBRIDGE TEXTS IN THE HISTORY OF PHILOSOPHY

Series editors

KARL AMERIKS

Professor of Philosophy at the University of Notre Dame

DESMOND M. CLARKE

Professor of Philosophy at University College Cork

The main objective of Cambridge Texts in the History of Philosophy is to expand the range, variety, and quality of texts in the history of philosophy which are available in English. The series includes texts by familiar names (such as Descartes and Kant) and also by less well-known authors. Wherever possible, texts are published in complete and unabridged form, and translations are specially commissioned for the series. Each volume contains a critical introduction together with a guide to further reading and any necessary glossaries and textual apparatus. The volumes are designed for student use at under-graduate and post-graduate level and will be of interest not only to students of philosophy, but also to a wider audience of readers in the history of science, the history of theology, and the history of ideas.

For a list of titles published in the series, please see end of book.

SØREN KIERKEGAARD

Fear and Trembling

EDITED BY

C. STEPHEN EVANS

Baylor University

AND

SYLVIA WALSH

Stetson University

TRANSLATED BY

SYLVIA WALSH

CAMBRIDGE
UNIVERSITY PRESS

CAMBRIDGE UNIVERSITY PRESS
Cambridge, New York, Melbourne, Madrid, Cape Town, Singapore, São Paulo

Cambridge University Press
The Edinburgh Building, Cambridge CB2 8RU, UK

Published in the United States of America by Cambridge
University Press, New York

www.cambridge.org
Information on this title: www.cambridge.org/9780521612692

First published 2006
Reprinted 2007 (twice)

Printed in the United Kingdom at the University Press, Cambridge

A catalogue record for this publication is available from the British Library

ISBN 978-0-521-84810-7 hardback
ISBN 978-0-521-61269-2 paperback

Contents

Introduction

Fear and Trembling, written when the author was only thirty years old, is in all likelihood Søren Kierkegaard's most-read book. This would not have surprised Kierkegaard, who wrote prophetically in his journal that "once I am dead, *Fear and Trembling* alone will be enough for an imperishable name as an author. Then it will [be] read, translated into foreign languages as well."[1] In one sense the book is not difficult to read. It is often assigned in introductory university classes, for it is the kind of book that a novice in philosophy can pick up and read with interest and profit – stimulating questions about ethics and God, faith and reason, experience and imagination. However, in another sense the book is profoundly difficult, the kind of book that can be baffling to the scholar who has read it many times and studied it for years – giving rise to a bewildering variety of conflicting interpretations.

Many of these interpretations have focused on the book's relation to Kierkegaard's own life, and in particular on the widely known story of Kierkegaard's broken engagement to Regine Olsen. There is little doubt that part of Kierkegaard's own motivation for writing *Fear and Trembling* was to present a disguised explanation to Regine of his true reasons for breaking off the engagement. However, it is just as certain that the philosophical importance of the book does not depend on these personal and biographical points; the book can be read and has been read with profit by those with no knowledge of Kierkegaard's own life.

---

[1] *Søren Kierkegaard's Journals and Papers*, vols. I–VII, ed. and trans. Howard V. Hong and Edna H. Hong (Bloomington, Ind.: Indiana University Press, 1967–78). Entry no. 6491 (vol. VI).

Fear and Trembling is described on the title page as a "dialectical lyric," and this description accurately captures its paradoxical character. On the one hand the book is indeed lyrical, with intensely poetical and moving passages that engage the imagination as well as the emotions of the reader. Poetic figures such as the "knight of faith," the "knight of infinite resignation," and the "tragic hero" move before the reader's eyes and take shape in story and myth. However, the book is also "dialectical" in the sense that it poses sharply defined philosophical and theological questions about such issues as the relation between a life of religious faith and the ethical life, and the relation between personal virtue and integrity and social and political duties.

Fear and Trembling takes as its point of departure the biblical story of the "binding of Isaac" from Genesis 22, in which God tests Abraham by asking him to sacrifice his son Isaac on Mount Moriah. Kierkegaard's book as a whole can best be described as a poetical and philosophical response to this biblical story. In the Genesis account Abraham shows his willingness to obey God, but at the last moment God sends an angel to stay his hand, and Abraham discovers a ram that he sacrifices in place of his son.

This story from the Hebrew Bible is reprised in the New Testament in Hebrews 11, where the "heroes of faith" are listed and described. Abraham has a prominent place in this list of exemplars; his action in being willing to sacrifice Isaac is singled out by the author of Hebrews in verses 17–19 as a key part of Abraham's story and a major reason why Abraham is a paradigm of faith. The book of Hebrews thus provides a clear illustration of the status Abraham enjoys for both Jews and Christians (as well as Muslims) as the "father of faith." There is a long tradition of commentary on this Genesis story, from both Jewish and Christian thinkers, and the questions the story raises seem no less relevant today than in previous centuries.

Among these questions some of the most pressing concern the relative value and danger of religious devotion as a source of action. *Fear and Trembling* shows a clear awareness that the story about Abraham's willingness to sacrifice Isaac is in many ways a dangerous narrative. We live in a world where religious fundamentalists try to justify violence against innocent people by appealing to what they perceive as God's commands. Deranged parents sometimes kill their children in the belief that they have been commanded by God to do so. *Fear and Trembling* rightly worries about people who may respond to the story in these kinds of ways, asking whether one should dare think about the Abraham story: "Can one then speak candidly about Abraham without running the risk that an individual in mental confusion might go and do likewise?" (p. 23) Religious faith seems to some people to be too dangerous to tolerate, something that leads to war, terrorism, and fanaticism. We can see this in John Lennon's famous line in his song "Imagine," where he dreams of a world where "there's no heaven, and no religion too." Though *Fear and Trembling* shows a deep understanding of this kind of worry about religious faith, it also tries to show that to lose the possibility of genuine faith is to lose something of incalculable value. To eliminate faith in order to eliminate fanaticism is to deify "the established social-political order." Such a secularized society might eliminate fanatics, but it would also eliminate such figures as a Martin Luther King, Jr., who mounted a religious critique of the established order. Most importantly from Kierkegaard's perspective, such a secularized society would remove any transcendent meaning that gives the lives of individual humans depth and value.

Who is the "author" of *Fear and Trembling?*

Kierkegaard's *Fear and Trembling* was published in Copenhagen in 1843 as part of an outpouring of pseudonymous books which he wrote at a furious pace, and most of which appeared in just three years between 1843 and 1846. Other books in this group include *Either/Or, Repetition, The Concept of Anxiety, Prefaces, Philosophical Fragments, Stages on Life's Way,* and *Concluding Unscientific Postscript.* At the same time as Kierkegaard was producing these pseudonymous books, he also published a series of devotional *Upbuilding Discourses* under his own name. The pseudonymous books are attributed to a variety of characters with names such as Victor Eremita (Victor the Hermit), Vigilius Haufniensis (The Watchman of Copenhagen), and Johannes Climacus (John the Climber). Thus, the name that appears on the title page of *Fear and Trembling* is not Kierkegaard's own, but "Johannes de silentio." This fact is of great importance.

Why did Kierkegaard employ these pseudonyms? Clearly it was not to preserve anonymity. Within a short time of the appearance of the first of these volumes the identity of the true author was widely known. In fact

Kierkegaard went so far as to put his own name on the title page as "editor" of two of the volumes, a move which clearly shows that he was not trying to hide his connection to the writings. The reasons for the pseudonyms lie in Kierkegaard's understanding of himself as a "Danish Socrates," who attempted to help his contemporaries discover truth for themselves, much as did the actual Socrates, who compared himself to a midwife who helped others give birth to ideas. Kierkegaard's pseudonyms can usefully be compared to characters in a novel, who have their own viewpoints and voices that may or may not overlap with those of the author of the novel. In creating the pseudonyms Kierkegaard attempts what he calls "indirect communication," which he sees as vital when one is dealing with moral and religious insights that bear directly on the self, and that can only be properly understood when personally appropriated. Kierkegaard does not didactically tell us what is what, but creates characters who embody various views of life and the self. The reader who encounters these characters is thus forced to think for himself or herself about the issues.

Virtually all Kierkegaard scholars today agree then that distinctions between the various pseudonyms, as well as the distinction between Kierkegaard and the pseudonyms, must be respected. It is a mistake to blend together passages from Johannes the seducer in *Either/Or* I, from Vigilius Haufniensis in *The Concept of Anxiety*, and from Johannes de silentio in *Fear and Trembling* as if they all reflect Kierkegaard's own views. Most scholars today therefore respect Kierkegaard's request to distinguish the words of the pseudonyms from those works he wrote under his own name: "Therefore if it should occur to anyone to want to quote a particular passage from the [pseudonymous] books, it is my wish, my prayer, that he will do me the kindness of citing the respective pseudonymous author's name, not mine . . ."[2] However, many textbook characterizations of Kierkegaard still ignore this literary dimension of his writings, and thus misinterpretations are common. A proper interpretation of *Fear and Trembling* must therefore try to understand the figure of Johannes de silentio. Unfortunately, all we can know about this Johannes must be derived from his book, and thus an understanding of his

---

[2] Søren Kierkegaard, *Concluding Unscientific Postscript*, ed. and trans. Howard V. Hong and Edna H. Hong (Princeton: Princeton University Press, 1992), p. 627. This passage occurs as part of "A First and Last Explanation" that Kierkegaard appended to this pseudonymous book under his own name.

standpoint as an author must go hand in hand with an understanding of the work itself.

One important clue in understanding the pseudonymous author may be the name itself: John of silence, silent John. Though Johannes is in one sense talkative, we shall see that at key points it is what he does not say that may be most important. Another clue may be found in the "Motto" from Johann Georg Hamann that appears at the beginning of the book: "What Tarquin the Proud communicated in his garden with the beheaded poppies was understood by the son but not by the messenger." The reference is to an ancient story of Rome in which the son of Tarquin, the king of Rome, had gained power in the rival city of Gabii. The son sent a messenger to his father to ask for advice about what he should do, but the father did not trust the messenger. Saying nothing, he simply walked around in the garden and struck the flowers off the tallest poppies. When the messenger related this behavior to the son, the son correctly inferred that he should try to bring about the death of the leading citizens of the city.

Mottos are by their nature enigmatic and suggestive, and one cannot be sure what is meant by this reference to the story. However, it certainly seems plausible that Johannes as the author of the book is himself the "messenger" in this case, and thus in some ways is communicating through his work something he himself does not fully understand. It is perhaps less clear who is the "father" from whom the message comes, and who is the "son" who is supposed to receive the message with understanding.

Imagining Abraham and Isaac

Fear and Trembling begins with an amusing preface that cleverly satirizes both modern philosophy and modern European culture in general, focusing on the concepts of doubt and faith. According to Johannes, everyone in the modern world has apparently doubted everything, just as everyone is supposed to possess genuine religious faith. Johannes is clearly not so enamored with these alleged achievements of modernity, which he, through irony, compares unfavorably with the practices of the ancient Greeks and early Christians. For the ancient Greeks, "proficiency in doubting is not achieved in a matter of days or weeks" (p. 4). Supposedly everyone in our age begins with the stance that those Greek philosophers worked a lifetime to achieve. In a similar manner, "in those olden days" faith was "a lifelong task," but modern people must "go further" since they all begin "where those venerable figures arrived" (p. 5). What do doubt and faith have in common? For Johannes they are both human activities, and he clearly thinks that neither is as easy as modernity assumes. Perhaps once the difficulties of these human tasks are appreciated, people will be less eager to "go further" to the intellectual challenges of the "System," the grand speculative attempt by the philosopher G. W. F. Hegel and his followers to understand the whole of nature and human history in terms of "Absolute Spirit."

After this satirical preface, Johannes offers us a section called "Tuning Up," a kind of lyrical prelude that consists of a series of imaginative variations on the biblical story of Abraham's willingness to sacrifice Isaac at God's command. It is clear that Johannes pays attention to this story about Abraham and Isaac because he wants to understand faith and looks to a universally recognized exemplar of faith for help. This fact provides a baseline insight that must be constantly kept in mind; *Fear and Trembling* is primarily a book about faith, not a book about ethics. However, even the discussion of faith is indirect in character. Johannes does not really tell us what faith is but what it is not, even though he says a lot about faith. He primarily helps us understand faith more clearly by distinguishing genuine faith from counterfeits and easily confused relatives and substitutes. The imaginative versions of the story that Johannes produces in "Tuning Up" all in some way picture an "Abraham" who differs from the biblical Abraham by lacking faith.

In the first variation, Johannes imagines an Abraham who tries to explain to Isaac that God requires him as a sacrifice, but who is unable to make Isaac understand. In response to Isaac's horror, Abraham pretends to Isaac to be a moral monster, an idolater who is going to sacrifice Isaac "because it is my desire" rather than because of God's command, telling himself that it would be better for Isaac to lose faith in Abraham than to lose his faith in the goodness of God (p. 9). In the second variation, everything is as it is in the biblical story, except that Abraham as a result of the experience "saw joy no more" (p. 9). As we shall see later, a crucial dimension of the actual Abraham is Abraham's joy, his ability to be happy with Isaac, trusting in God's promise. In the third version Abraham decides that he is wrong to have been willing to sacrifice Isaac and repents, but finds himself vacillating in his repentance, unsure that it was a sin "to have been willing to sacrifice to God the best he owned," but worried that if it was a sin, "how could it be forgiven, for what sin was more grievous?" (p. 10) In the fourth and final version, Abraham draws the knife, but his "left hand was clenched in despair" and "a shudder went through his body," and as a result Isaac, who has observed this, loses his faith (p. 10).

All these imagined stories are related by a man (perhaps Johannes himself) who is transfixed by the story of Abraham and Isaac, a man who seems obsessed with understanding Abraham, but whose energetic intellectual strivings only show him more clearly how difficult, perhaps impossible, the task is. Every time the man returns home from one of his imaginative pilgrimages to Mount Moriah, he collapses "from fatigue," and says: "Surely no one was as great as Abraham. Who is able to understand him?" (p. 11) The point of the variations clearly lies in their differences from the Abraham story. The alternative "Abrahams" are in some way, unlike the actual Abraham, understandable; in looking at them we understand Abraham better in the sense that we know better what faith is not.

"Tuning Up" is followed by "A Tribute to Abraham," which tells the story of the actual biblical Abraham as a person of faith, again interspersing the tale with imaginative variations on the story. Johannes sets the story in context, beginning with Abraham's willingness to emigrate from the land of his fathers to a foreign country and continuing with God's promise to make of Abraham's descendants a mighty nation. This promise is one that Abraham believes despite having no child of Sarah his wife until he is a hundred years old. This context makes the test to which God puts Abraham by asking for the sacrifice of Isaac seem all the more pointless and absurd. How can God's pledge that Isaac will be the child through which God fulfills his promise to Abraham be fulfilled if Abraham is himself going to end Isaac's life?

Several themes dominate Johannes' version of the story. One is that Abraham's faith requires him to believe what is preposterous or absurd. This is not only true for Abraham's willingness to sacrifice Isaac, but is present from the very beginning of Abraham's story. When he left the land of his fathers, "he left one thing behind and took one thing with him. He left his worldly understanding behind and took faith with him; otherwise he undoubtedly would not have emigrated but surely would have thought it preposterous" (p. 14). Note that there is a perspectival dimension to this claim. Faith is said to be absurd from the perspective of "worldly understanding," and this leaves open the possibility that things look different from the perspective of faith. Since Johannes himself repeatedly says that he does not possess faith, this may explain why Johannes has so much difficulty in understanding Abraham.

A second dimension of the story that Johannes emphasizes is that Abraham's faith is a "this-worldly" faith. Christian theologians traditionally have held that faith involves not only a belief that God exists, but a belief that God is good, and hence can be trusted, following Hebrews 11:6: "And without faith it is impossible to please God, for whoever would approach him must believe that he exists and that he rewards those who seek him."[3] So Johannes emphasizes that Abraham believes in God's promises and has an expectation of happiness and joy, and for Johannes God's goodness must be understood in relation to our earthly, temporal lives. Because he is a person of faith, Abraham gives us no "song of sorrow" (p. 15). "Abraham believed and believed for this life" (p. 17). He did not merely believe that after death he would experience God's goodness and be rewarded for his faithfulness, but that "he would grow old in the land, honored by the people, blessed by posterity, forever remembered in Isaac, his dearest one in life" (p. 17).

A faith that only pertains to some other world is not really faith at all, says Johannes, "but only the remotest possibility of faith, which faintly spies its object at the edge of the horizon yet is separated from it by a yawning abyss within which despair plays its tricks" (p. 17). In some ways this characterization of faith as something dimly and distantly recognized fits Johannes himself. He explicitly says that his own "faith" resembles this kind of "other-worldly faith," and thus we may here have an account of how Johannes can say some true things about faith, insofar as he "faintly spies its object at the edge of the horizon" and yet in many ways does not understand faith at all. As we shall see, what is distinctive about Abraham as a person of faith is not his willingness to sacrifice Isaac at God's command. He shares that trait with several other characters who lack faith. What is distinctive about Abraham's faith shows itself in his joyful ability to "receive Isaac back" and resume ordinary life with him, trusting in God's promises.

---

[3] *The New Oxford Annotated Bible*, 3rd edn. (Oxford: Oxford University Press, 2001), new revised standard version.

Faith and infinite resignation

The bulk of *Fear and Trembling* is devoted to three philosophical "Problems" that Johannes poses, but before settling down to philosophical business, he provides a kind of extended preface to this section of the book, which he entitles "A Preliminary Outpouring from the Heart" (in Walsh's free but insightful translation). This "outpouring" is dominated by two ideal figures, whom Johannes designates as "the knight of infinite resignation" and the "knight of faith." Both of these knights, according to Johannes, have made what he calls the "movement of infinite resignation." Resignation is a willingness to sacrifice the whole of the finite world, all that a person values in this life, for the sake of what Johannes variously calls "the infinite," "the eternal," or "God."

Johannes illustrates infinite resignation by picturing a young man whose identity is completely concentrated in his love for a princess; this youth has the strength "to concentrate the whole content of life and the meaning of actuality into one single wish" (pp. 35–36). The love turns out to be one that cannot be consummated in time, and this young man shows himself to be a knight of infinite resignation by renouncing his temporal hopes for happiness with the princess: instead,

> the love for that princess became for him the expression of an eternal love, assumed a religious character, was transfigured into a love of the eternal being, which to be sure denied the fulfillment of the love but still reconciled him once again in the eternal consciousness of its validity in an eternal form that no actuality can take from him. (pp. 36–37)

Infinite resignation then embodies a kind of other-worldly religiousness, a life-stance that Johannes himself claims to understand and even to be able to realize. Johannes is "convinced that God is love," but God's love for him is "incommensurable with the whole of actuality" (p. 28). As a result he does not relate to God in the details of his life: "I do not trouble God with my petty cares" (p. 28). If Johannes himself had been asked to sacrifice Isaac, he affirms that he would have been willing to obey and make the sacrifice, but at the expense of any happiness in time: "Now all is lost; God demands Isaac, I sacrifice him and with him all my joy – yet God is love and continues to be that for me, for in temporality God and I cannot converse, we have no language in common" (p. 29). Johannes knows that some people might confuse his "immense resignation" with faith, but he knows that such resignation is just a substitute for faith. The difference between the two shows itself in their respective post-trial attitudes towards Isaac:

> What came easiest for Abraham would have been difficult for me – once again to be joyful with Isaac! – for whoever has made the infinite movement with all the infinity of his soul, of his own accord and on his own responsibility, and cannot do more only keeps Isaac with pain. (p. 29)

Infinite resignation by itself is a substitute for faith, and yet Johannes also describes it as an ingredient in faith: "Infinite resignation is the last stage before faith, so that whoever has not made this movement does not have faith" (p. 39). Abraham has then made the movement of infinite resignation, but resignation is not what is distinctive about his faith. Rather that distinctiveness is found in the "second movement" by which the person of faith, having resigned the whole of the finite, receives it all back again. Abraham, "by a double movement ... had regained his original condition and therefore received Isaac more joyfully than the first time" (p. 29). Johannes describes this second movement as made possible by a faith or belief[4] "by virtue of the absurd" (p. 30).

This joy in the finite makes it difficult to recognize the genuine "knight of faith," for in his external appearance he bears a suspicious resemblance to a "bourgeois-philistine" who simply lives for the finite. Johannes imagines such a knight of faith, and finds himself taken aback: "Dear me! Is this the person, is it actually him? He looks just like a tax collector" (p. 32). The knight of faith's footing "is sturdy, belonging entirely to finitude" (p. 32). Johannes pictures the knight of faith as imagining a wonderful roast lamb dinner he believes his wife has made for him; if she really has the dinner, "to see him eat would be an enviable sight for distinguished people and an inspiring one for the common man, for his appetite is heartier than Esau's" (p. 33). Yet if the wife does not have the dinner, he is not disappointed. Somehow the knight of faith has made "the movement of infinity" by "renouncing everything," and "yet the finite tastes every bit as good to him as to someone who never knew anything higher" (p. 34). In the same way, Abraham has given up Isaac

---

[4] Danish has but one word, *tro*, for both English terms.

to God and yet is able to receive him back with joy; in fact he expected all along to receive him back with joy.

What exactly does Abraham believe? What does he think as he rides to Mount Moriah with Isaac and the knife? Commentators have found this a difficult question. On the one hand, Abraham knows, says Johannes, that Isaac is to die by his own hand: "at the decisive moment he must know what he himself will do" (p. 105). Yet Johannes insists that Abraham continues to believe "by virtue of the absurd" that God will not in fact require Isaac of him: "He climbed the mountain, and even at the moment when the knife gleamed he believed – that God would not demand Isaac" (p. 29).

One could of course simply take this as implying that Abraham has a contradictory belief, that he believes both that Isaac will die and that he will not die. However, it is unclear what such a contradictory belief would amount to or whether it would have any clear meaning at all. Psychologically, the only way such a contradictory belief would be possible would be if Abraham were self-deceived in some way, so that he could have a belief without realizing that he had it and therefore also could have a contradictory one. It is certain that Johannes does not think of Abraham in this way, for there would be nothing admirable about such a confused, or self-deceptive, contradictory belief.

Does Abraham then believe that God will not in fact require him to sacrifice Isaac? Has he guessed that this is "only a trial," cleverly discerning that he must play his part and appear to be willing to do something that he knows he in fact will not have to do? We have just quoted a passage in which Johannes does attribute to Abraham the belief that God will not in fact demand Isaac of him. However, it cannot be right to picture Abraham as someone who has cleverly figured out how to play along with God's game, so to speak. For one thing Johannes says explicitly that the rightness of Abraham's act and its greatness cannot be a function of the outcome (p. 55). Abraham, says Johannes, does not know what the outcome will be, and thus we cannot emulate him if we interpret the story in light of the result. When Abraham begins to act he does not know the result, and if we wish to be people of faith we must put ourselves in his shoes, so to speak, and also be willing to act without knowing what the results of our actions will be. If we imagine Abraham acting because he has craftily figured out what the outcome will be, Johannes' comments here make no sense.

Johannes actually goes to some pains to distinguish Abraham's faith from "worldly wisdom," the calculations of human probability, which even infinite resignation has already transcended (p. 31). Faith is not merely a vague hope that this or that could possibly happen if something else happens. For example, Johannes distinguishes faith from one of its "caricatures," which he describes as a "paltry hope" that says "One can't know what will happen, it still might be possible" (pp. 30–31).

Yet we should remember that caricatures do contain a likeness to what they are caricaturing, and there is something in such vague hope that bears a resemblance to faith. Johannes does picture Abraham as uncertain about what is going to happen. Though Abraham definitely knows what he is going to do, says Johannes, he also believes that "surely it will not happen, or if it does, the Lord will give me a new Isaac, namely by virtue of the absurd" (p. 101). What is the difference between this attitude on the part of Abraham and what we might call a clever Abraham, a worldly wise Abraham?

I think there are two differences and one similarity between the genuine Abraham and a clever Abraham. The similarity has just been pointed out: it lies in the fact that Abraham does indeed have some uncertainty about what is going to happen. One might say that some of what he knows and believes consists of conditionals. He knows, for example, that he will sacrifice Isaac *if* God does not revoke the command. Obviously, this kind of conditional belief or knowledge suggests that there is some possibility that God could revoke the command and that Abraham is aware of this possibility. To that extent such an attitude looks like the "paltry hope" mentioned above. Yet there are two important differences.

The first difference lies in the ground of the hope. The "paltry hope" that Johannes describes as a caricature of faith is grounded in human experience, which gives us our sense of what is probable and what is possible. Faith, however, has an entirely different ground. Johannes is enigmatic in describing faith's ground; perhaps since he lacks faith himself he does not fully understand what this ground is. However, one thing is clear. He consistently says that faith holds to various possibilities "by virtue of the absurd," and he is clear that someone who looks at things from this viewpoint of the absurd has completely rejected human calculative reasoning. On the contrary, faith requires a clear-headed understanding that from the perspective of human experience the situation appears impossible. The knight of faith therefore acknowledges the impossibility and at the same moment believes the absurd, for if he imagines himself to have faith without acknowledging the impossibility with all the passion of his soul and with his whole heart, then he deceives himself . . . (p. 40)

Abraham's mental state seems complex. Johannes says that throughout the time of his testing, "he [Abraham] believed; he believed that God would not demand Isaac of him, while he still was willing to sacrifice him if it was demanded. He believed by virtue of the absurd, for human calculation was out of the question. . . ." (p. 29).

The second clear difference between faith and this "paltry hope" that is its caricature is that faith has a kind of confidence and sureness that worldly shrewdness lacks. At bottom calculative shrewdness in this case would be irrational, for it amounts to believing something *will* happen that one knows to be highly improbable merely on the grounds that it is possible. Such a hope can never be free of doubts. However, Abraham, according to Johannes, "believed and did not doubt" (p. 17). Is Abraham's belief also irrational? It certainly is from the viewpoint of worldly wisdom, and Johannes often describes faith from that viewpoint as believing what is "preposterous" (p. 17). Yet it also seems clear that things do not appear that way to Abraham himself. I have already quoted the passage in which Johannes says that when Abraham emigrated from his native land, he "left his worldly understanding behind and took faith with him; otherwise he undoubtedly would not have emigrated but surely would have thought it preposterous" (p. 14). The Danish term for preposterous here is *urimeligt*, which could also be translated as "unreasonable." If Abraham had not had faith, then he would have seen his actions as unreasonable; with faith it is clearly a different matter.

But what exactly is Abraham confident of? I think the answer can only be that Abraham is confident that God will keep his promises. For Abraham, as for Johannes, God is love, God is good. However, for Abraham, unlike Johannes, God's goodness must translate into the concerns of daily, temporal life. Abraham, says Johannes, had "received the promise that in his seed all the generations of the world would be blessed," and Abraham believes that God will fulfill this promise in Isaac, even if Abraham does not understand how God will do this or even how it is possible (p. 14). This does not mean that Abraham knew for sure that God would do what he in fact did, i.e. revoke the command to sacrifice Isaac. Johannes pictures Abraham as a man who simply rests in his confidence that God will fulfill the promise without knowing exactly how this will come about.

Johannes does picture Abraham as thinking that it is *possible* that God may not require him to make the sacrifice. However, he does not know this will happen, and he does not count on it happening, but is willing to go through with the sacrifice if that is required. Even if he does sacrifice Isaac, he believes God will fulfill his promises. Humanly speaking, this is indeed irrational, but Johannes makes it clear that Abraham does not evaluate his actions from this perspective. In a clear allusion to the writer of Hebrews' reading of the story, who makes this point central in Hebrews 11:17–19, Johannes says that Abraham could actually have carried out the sacrifice, because Abraham believed that God could raise Isaac from the dead, if that were necessary to fulfill God's promise that Isaac would be the father of many nations:

> Let us go further. We let Isaac actually be sacrificed. Abraham believed. He did not believe that he would be blessed one day in the hereafter but that he would become blissfully happy here in the world. God could give him a new Isaac, call the sacrificed one back to life. He believed by virtue of the absurd, for all human calculation had long since ceased. (pp. 29–30)

I conclude that Abraham does not, at the crucial time, hold the contradictory belief that he will and will not sacrifice Isaac. Nor is his mental state that of the shrewd person who has used experience to figure out the outcome and adjust his behavior accordingly. Rather, Abraham simply rests unwaveringly in his trust in God's goodness; he believes that God will keep his promise to him in this life, even though he does not know exactly how God will do this, and realizes that from the perspective of human experience it looks impossible.

The knight of faith vs. the tragic hero

After the "Preliminary Outpouring" Johannes launches into the philosophical meat of *Fear and Trembling*, which consists of detailed discussions of three philosophical problems. The first problem posed (Is there a teleological suspension of the ethical?) is closely related to the second (Is there an absolute duty to God?). To ask whether there is such a thing as a "teleological suspension of the ethical" is to ask whether "the ethical" represents the highest task for humans, or whether there might be something, such as a relation to God that might involve "an absolute duty to God," that is "higher" than the ethical and for which the ethical could rightly be suspended. Johannes argues that if Abraham's willingness to sacrifice Isaac is justifiable or admirable, then one must affirm that there is indeed such a thing as a "teleological suspension of the ethical" and that Abraham does indeed have an absolute duty to God that trumps his ethical duty.

To understand Johannes' discussion of these questions (as well as his third problem) it is crucial to understand clearly what he means by "the ethical," since for some philosophers ethical duties are simply defined as a person's highest obligations, and the question of whether there could be a higher obligation than the highest makes no sense. For example, if someone accepts a "divine command" account of moral obligations, which claims (in one version) that all moral obligations are divine commands, and that whatever God commands thereby becomes a moral obligation, then Abraham, if commanded by God to sacrifice Isaac, has a moral or ethical obligation to do so.[5] The idea that his obligation to obey God might be a higher obligation that would trump his ethical obligation would on this view be nonsensical.

So what does Johannes mean by "the ethical?" Johannes often describes the ethical as identical with "the universal," and this term suggests to many a Kantian conception of the ethical, since Kant identifies moral obligations with those imperatives that can be universalized: "The ethical as such is the universal, and as the universal it applies to everyone, which may be expressed from another angle by saying that it is in force at every moment" (p. 46). However, this use of Kantian language is not decisive, since Hegel also appropriates this language for his own purposes.

The differences between Kant and Hegel are crucial for understanding what Johannes has in mind by "the ethical" when he denies that faith can be understood in ethical terms. For Kant the fundamental precepts of morality apply directly to individuals as rational beings; ultimately our

---

[5] I believe that Kierkegaard himself does accept this view of moral obligations and thus has a different view of the ethical than does Johannes de silentio. See my *Kierkegaard's Ethic of Love: Divine Commands and Moral Obligations* (Oxford: Oxford University Press, 2004). For an extended explanation and defense of a divine command theory of moral obligation, see Robert Adams, *Finite and Infinite Goods* (Oxford: Oxford University Press, 1999). I do not, by the way, make a distinction between morality and ethics as some philosophers such as Hegel do, and I do not believe that Kierkegaard accepts such a distinction either.

knowledge of morality must be a priori and not derived from experience. Each of us can grasp the "categorical imperative" by the use of reason and apply it for himself or herself as a touchstone to evaluate concrete moral duties. For Hegel, however, Kant's categorical imperative is overly formal and cannot guide human beings to act in particular situations. Rather, for Hegel the demands of reason must become embodied in the laws and customs of a people. The individual satisfies the demands of reason not by legislating for himself or herself, but by recognizing and affirming the rational character of the customs and laws of society. This higher social ethic is called by Hegel *Sittlichkeit*, and it is *Sittlichkeit* that Johannes has in mind when he affirms that if Abraham is not to be condemned then there must be something higher than the ethical, something higher than the customs and laws of a society.

That Johannes has something like Hegelian *Sittlichkeit* in mind when he speaks of the ethical is clear when one examines the actual characteristics of the ethical. Those characteristics are best seen in the character Johannes calls the "tragic hero," who is described by him as the "beloved son of ethics" (p. 99). Johannes gives three examples of the tragic hero from antiquity, all of which bear a superficial resemblance to Abraham. Agamemnon sacrifices Iphigenia so as to make it possible for the Greeks to sail to Troy. Jephthah, in the Old Testament, in order to secure a victory for ancient Israel, vows to sacrifice the first creature he sees when he returns from the battle, and that creature turns out to be his daughter. Brutus, an early consul of Rome, had his sons executed for treason when they participated in a conspiracy to restore the former king.

Each one of these tragic heroes, says Johannes, "remains within the ethical." Each "lets an expression of the ethical have its telos in a higher expression of the ethical" (p. 51). This is quite right from the point of view of Hegelian ethics, which sees duties as linked to the social institutions people participate in and views the state and the duties associated with it as higher than the duties linked to participation in family life. These tragic heroes, like Abraham, are called to sacrifice children, but the sacrifices in their case are for the sake of a higher ethical end or telos, which relativizes their familial duties. The sacrifices are justifiable and understandable to others in society (a point Johannes discusses at length in Problem III).

One can see that for Johannes there is an historical and cultural component to what is "ethical." Ethical duties are not derived from some timeless rational principle, as would be the case for Kant, but from the concrete customs of a people. When Johannes says that "everyone" can understand and approve of the actions of his tragic heroes, he clearly means everyone in their respective societies. Jephthah's actions were consistent with the views of his society, understandable and justifiable to his contemporaries, but one would have a difficult time finding an ethicist today who would approve of someone executing a child because that person had rashly promised to sacrifice the first creature he saw on returning from a battle.

Some people (Kantians, for example) might think this is a very inadequate conception of the ethical life, and if it is an inadequate conception of the ethical life, one might conclude that *Fear and Trembling* itself suffers from a deep flaw. Perhaps if the primary purpose of the book were to develop an account of ethics, this would be a flaw. However, as I have already argued, *Fear and Trembling* is not a book about ethics; it is a book about faith. The ethical life is discussed because Johannes thinks that his contemporaries are likely to confuse what they thought of as ethics with faith, and he thinks it is important that faith be distinguished from the ethical life in this sense. If that is his major purpose, then it is logical that Johannes should employ the conception of the ethical life that he believes is pervasive in his own society, whether that view of the ethical life is correct or not. This is so even if Kierkegaard himself holds a different view of the true ethical life.

There is little doubt that Kierkegaard himself saw Hegel's philosophy as the dominant view among his intellectual peers, and that fact alone, along with the many jabs at Hegel in *Fear and Trembling*, gives one reason to think that Hegelianism might be the main target of the book. One might object that this is an overestimation of the importance and pervasiveness of Hegelianism. However, Kierkegaard himself did not view Hegelianism as merely an esoteric intellectual view; he saw it as an intellectual expression of the kind of society he saw around him in Europe, the society that he called "Christendom." Kierkegaard tells us that he saw his own mission as the "introduction of Christianity into Christendom."[6]

[6] See, for example, *"The Single Individual": Two Notes Concerning My Work as An Author*, published in *The Point of View for My Work as an Author*, ed. and trans. Howard V. Hong and Edna H. Hong (Princeton: Princeton University Press, 1998), pp. 102–26, especially 123–4, and also p. 42 in *The Point of View for My Work as an Author*.

What does Kierkegaard mean by "Christendom" and why is it a problem? Christendom, according to Kierkegaard, embodies the "enormous illusion" that "we are all Christians" as a matter of course.[7] In such a situation being a Christian is simply identified with being a nice person, a good Dane, or a good European, the kind of person who lives respectably and fulfills his or her social roles and responsibilities. In short, being a Christian is identified with someone who has actualized "the ethical" in the sense of *Sittlichkeit*. Hegel and the Hegelians did in fact see the cultures of western Europe as the culmination of the development of "Absolute Spirit." One could actually say that Hegel saw modern Western culture as the coming of the kingdom of God on earth, and thus the citizen who participated in its *Sittlichkeit* was also a member of that kingdom.

The practical and exoteric complacency about Christian faith that Kierkegaard sees in the society around him, where it is assumed that every Dane is a Christian (unless that Dane happens to be Jewish), is thus the perfect counterpart to the esoteric philosophy of Hegel. On this Hegelian view, God is no longer a metaphysical abstraction but a concrete reality, actualized in human community. On such a view everyone has faith, and this helps to explain Johannes' barbs against the people of his own day who have already achieved the highest tasks and thus need to "go further" than faith to something difficult and significant.

Hegel claims that his own philosophy is Christian, and his Danish followers, such as the theologian H. L. Martensen, certainly claimed to be Christians. As Christian thinkers they are of course conversant with the biblical narrative about Abraham and see themselves as defenders of biblical faith. Johannes' argument leads to conclusions that put such thinkers in a tight spot. Faith, he says, involves the paradox that "the single individual is higher than the universal," a view that is incompatible with *Sittlichkeit*, which must judge an individual who violates social norms as sinning (p. 47). What does Johannes mean in saying faith involves such a "paradox?" He does not mean, I think, that faith requires a belief in what is logically contradictory. Rather, faith requires a belief that makes no sense from the point of view of "worldly wisdom," a belief that contradicts what appears to be the case. Normally, a person who deviates from social norms is just a bad person. Abraham may *appear* to

---

[7] See *The Point of View for My Work as an Author*, pp. 42–3.

be such a person, but, paradoxically, according to Johannes, actually represents something higher than the ethical.

This creates a problem for the Hegelian who claims that "the universal" is the highest, but who also wants to continue to honor Abraham as "the father of faith." Johannes says that "if this [recognizing the single individual as higher than the universal] is not faith, then Abraham is lost and faith has never existed in the world precisely because it has always existed" (p. 47). In other words, faith as a rare and admirable quality for which Abraham serves as a notable exemplar does not exist because faith has been identified with the commonplace quality of conforming to the norms of one's own society.

What is at stake here, theologically speaking, is the transcendence of God. Is God a real person, capable of communicating to and having a relation with God's human creatures? Or is the term "God" simply a symbol for what is regarded as "divine," the highest and truest values that lie at the heart of a particular social order? In Problem II Johannes says that in the latter case, "if I say . . . that it is my duty to love God, I am really only stating a tautology insofar as 'God' here is understood in an entirely abstract sense as the divine, i.e. the universal, i.e. the duty" (p. 59). This means that "God becomes an invisible vanishing point, an impotent thought" (p. 59). If Abraham's faith is to make any sense, God must be a transcendent personal reality. A relationship with God must be "the highest good" for the sake of which the socially assigned roles that make up "the ethical" are relativized (teleologically suspended). There can be duties to such a God that are not reducible to the duties given by one's human social relations.

That Johannes' target is Christendom and its Hegelian rationalization is confirmed by his discussions of Problems I and II. Immediately after raising the philosophical questions (Is there a teleological suspension of the ethical? Is there an absolute duty to God?) he makes it clear that the issues do not merely concern Abraham but have direct relevance to Christian faith. In Problem I Johannes cites Mary the mother of Jesus as an analogue to Abraham. Mary also receives and believes a message from God, one that makes no sense to her contemporaries, and which requires her to be "the single individual," since "the angel appeared only to Mary, and no one could understand her" (p. 57). In reality, Johannes suggests that all of the followers of Jesus are essentially in Abraham's situation:

> One is moved, one returns to those beautiful times when sweet,
> tender longings lead one to the goal of one's desire, to see Christ
> walking about in the promised land. One forgets the anxiety, the
> distress, the paradox. Was it so easy a matter not to make a mistake?
> Was it not appalling that this person who walked among others was
> God? Was it not terrifying to sit down to eat with him? (p. 58)

Nor are things any different for Christians in Johannes' day. To be a
Christian is to believe God communicates through a particular historical
individual, a message that always transcends *Sittlichkeit* and can come
into conflict with it, forcing the person of faith to be "the single individual" who breaks with established ways of thinking. It is only "the
outcome, the eighteen centuries" that fraudulently gives the illusion
that faith is easier today than it was for Abraham.

   That Johannes is using the figure of Abraham to send a message to
Christendom is even clearer in Problem II, where he quickly moves from
Abraham to a discussion of Luke 14:26, which represents Jesus as saying:
"If anyone comes to me and does not hate his own father and mother
and wife and children and brothers and sisters, yes, even his own life,
he cannot be my disciple." No sharper challenge to the reduction of
Christian faith to social and familial roles can be imagined, and we can
clearly see Abraham's absolute devotion to God as an analogue to the
Christian's devotion to God in Christ, a devotion that relativizes all
finite, earthly values.

   Johannes is well aware of the dangers of a faith that is not subject to
society's rules. He knows that some are "apprehensive of letting people
loose for fear that the worst will happen once the single individual deigns
to behave as the single individual" (p. 65). He acknowledges the dangers
of subjectivity, but he thinks there is a worse danger, namely that the
established social order will deify itself, eliminating the possibility that a
Socrates or a Jesus, a Gandhi or a Martin Luther King, Jr., could, as the
single individual, challenge that social order in response to an authentic
message from God.

   Johannes does acknowledge the need to establish criteria to help
us distinguish the genuine knight of faith from the fanatic (p. 65).
Commentators will disagree about the adequacy of the criteria he provides,
but I believe at least one of them is valuable. The fanatic, according to
Johannes, will be a "sectarian" who tries to form a party or faction to
buttress his views. (Today we might go beyond "sectarian" and think of

this fanatic as someone who might want to form a terrorist cell.) The genuine person of faith is, according to Johannes, "a witness, never a teacher" (p. 70). I think he means by this that a genuine person of faith will rely on the power of his or her moral example, and would never try to impose any views on others in a doctrinaire or manipulative way, much less employ violence to force others to conform to his or her way of thinking.[8]

Why Abraham cannot explain his action

Problem III poses the question: "Was it ethically defensible of Abraham to conceal his undertaking from Sarah, from Eliezer, from Isaac?" Johannes' answer to the question seems complex. Abraham, as Johannes tells the story, does not really explain what he is doing to anyone, including those such as Sarah and Isaac, who surely have a legitimate interest in the case. Is this silence justifiable or does it imply that there is something morally dubious about Abraham's actions?

Johannes argues that Abraham's actions are not *ethically* justifiable for reasons that are now clear. For Johannes language and reasoning are social activities. A person's ability to explain and justify an action requires socially accepted standards of what counts as right and what counts as rational. Insofar as Abraham's actions are rooted in a word from God that is not mediated through society, Abraham cannot possibly explain or justify his actions. He does not speak, not because he wishes to hide his actions; he would like nothing better than to explain himself, to gain relief by appealing to "the universal." He does not speak because regardless of what he says he cannot make himself understood, for if he could his actions would be an expression of *Sittlichkeit* after all. Abraham may be justified if there is indeed such a thing as faith, but he is not justified as an ethical figure (in Johannes' sense) and he cannot justify himself by appealing to existing social standards.

In Problem III Johannes gives numerous examples of mythical and literary figures who in some way shed light on Abraham, discussing such legends as Agnes and the merman, Faust, other literary examples such as

---

[8] For a powerful example of someone who uses the Abraham and Isaac story in the cause of peace, see Wilfred Owen's poem, "The Parable of the Old Man and the Young." Owen was a British poet who wrote during World War I, and the poem can be found in *The Poems of Wilfred Owen*, ed. Jon Stallworthy (New York and London: W. W. Norton, 1985), p. 151. I thank Sylvia Walsh for calling my attention to this poem.

Shakespeare's Gloucester (Richard III), and many others besides. Partly Johannes uses these figures once again to clarify what faith is by distinguishing it from look-alikes. However, he also uses them to open up a different issue altogether: why is the figure of Abraham important anyway? Why is it so vital to safeguard the possibility of faith as something distinct from the ethical? Earlier in the book he had already hinted at this theme. If Abraham had been an ethical figure, a tragic hero who killed himself rather than sacrifice Isaac, then "he would have been admired in the world, and his name would not be forgotten; but it is one thing to be admired, another to become a guiding star that rescues the anguished" (pp. 17–18). Who are the anguished ones, and how is it that Abraham's example can save them?

In his discussion of Problem III Johannes pictures several anguished souls. One is the merman taken from the legend of Agnes and the merman. Johannes varies the story by giving "the merman a human consciousness" and he asks us to "let his being a merman denote a human pre-existence in whose consequences his life was ensnared" (p. 84). The merman suffers because of his sin, which has consequences that cannot simply be undone and ignored, and which block the merman from simply "following the universal" and getting married. If the merman is to have Agnes, he must, like Abraham, "have recourse to the paradox. For when the single individual by his guilt has come outside the universal, he can only return to it by virtue of having come as the single individual into an absolute relation to the absolute" (p. 86).

Johannes underscores this observation by going on to "make an observation by which I say more than is said at any point previously" (p. 86). The sentences that follow have been regarded by more than one commentator as the key to understanding the whole book:

> Sin is not the first immediacy; sin is a later immediacy. In sin the single individual is already higher, in the direction of the demonic paradox, than the universal, because it is a contradiction for the universal to want to require itself of one who lacks the necessary condition … An ethics that ignores sin is an altogether futile discipline, but if it asserts sin, then it is for that very reason beyond itself. (p. 86)

Johannes further emphasizes the point by attaching a footnote, in which he affirms that in his discussion of Abraham he has deliberately avoided any reference to the question of sin and its reality . . . As soon as sin is introduced, ethics runs aground precisely upon repentance, for repentance is the highest ethical expression but precisely as such the deepest ethical self-contradiction. (p. 86)

Johannes seems to suggest that for some people the path to authentic selfhood lies in achieving the universal, taking up the social roles, and fulfilling the social duties allotted to them. However, there are others, such as the merman, who are "demonic" figures for whom "normal life" is not an option. Shakespeare's Gloucester is interpreted by Johannes as one of these people who simply are unable to tread the well-worn paths of "the ethical." Gloucester is a demonic figure who burns with resentment at the pity extended to him for his physical deformity, and according to Johannes, "Natures like Gloucester's cannot be saved by mediating them into an idea of society. Ethics really only makes a fool of them" (p. 93). Anguished people like this are doomed if there is no other path to authentic selfhood than to take up "my station and its duties," to use F. H. Bradley's apt summation of *Sittlichkeit*.

Who are these anguished people? Are they rare exceptions? People like Gloucester are undoubtedly exceptional. Johannes says explicitly that such people have been "placed outside the universal by nature or historical circumstance," and that this factor, which is "the beginning of the demonic," is one for which the individual "is not personally to blame" (p. 93). However, there is one important respect in which such people resemble us all, at least from the perspective of Christianity. From the perspective of orthodox Christian theology, sin is the universal human condition, not a status occupied by a few people who are excluded from society. Sin, according to Johannes, is also a condition that places us "outside the universal," though it is not a condition in which there is no personal blame. Kierkegaard's next book after *Fear and Trembling* is, significantly, *The Concept of Anxiety*, an exploration of the meaning of original sin and its psychological preconditions.

If original sin accurately describes the human condition, then no human being becomes an authentic self merely by conforming to *Sittlichkeit*. All of us may not be demonic figures, but all of us are in some ways among "the anguished ones" for whom Abraham may provide a guiding star. The highest good for every individual is a relation to God, a relation made possible by faith and which in turn makes possible a healing transformation of the person of faith. Johannes, we must remember, is not himself a person of faith and does not write from an explicitly Christian perspective, and so we get no more from him than these tantalizing observations. But it seems highly plausible that for Kierkegaard himself, all of us should see ourselves as like the merman and Gloucester in one important respect. All of us are in need of a healing of self that can only be made possible by faith, in which, like Abraham, an individual has "an absolute relation to the absolute" (p. 48). We are not all predisposed by natural or historical circumstances to become demonic, but we are, according to the doctrine of original sin, in some way predisposed to lose our way as human beings.

The general thrust of Protestant liberal thought from Kant to Hegel had been to understand genuine religious faith in ethical terms. Kant himself had closely linked true religious faith to the ethical life: "*Apart from a good life-conduct, anything which the human being supposes that he can do to become well-pleasing to God is mere religious delusion and counterfeit service of God.*"[9] When Kantian ethics is converted by Hegel to *Sittlichkeit* then the equation of faith with the ethical sets the stage for the triumph of Christendom and the identification of religious faith with social conformism.

Kierkegaard was convinced that the reduction of the life of faith to the ethical life was disastrous, because it eliminated any solution to the fundamental problem posed by the ethical life: the problem of guilt. Kant had himself posed the issue as sharply as anyone else in *Religion within the Boundaries of Mere Reason*, but it is by no means clear that he had solved it.[10] Kierkegaard thinks that genuine faith requires an individual relation with God that is personally transformative. Each person can become "the single individual" who can become an authentic self by responding in faith to God's call on that individual. Such a faith is not reducible to fulfilling one's social roles but can be the basis of a renewal of the self and those social institutions. The person who has experienced this kind of transformative faith will feel no need to "go further" than faith.

A faith in a transcendent God of course raises many important philosophical questions. Faith that such a God has become incarnate as a

---

[9] Immanuel Kant, *Religion within the Boundaries of Mere Reason*, ed. and trans. Allen Wood and George Di Giovanni, with an introduction by Robert Merrihew Adams (Cambridge: Cambridge University Press, 1998), p. 166 (emphasis Kant's).
[10] See John Hare, *The Moral Gap* (Oxford: Oxford University Press, 1996), for a strong argument that Kantian ethics itself demands a solution to the problem of guilt beyond that offered by Kant.

particular human being raises even more questions. Most of these questions are not resolved in *Fear and Trembling*. But then Johannes does not want to make faith easy for us. However, if we do not accurately understand the nature of faith, those questions cannot even be posed. Difficulties that are not recognized cannot be dealt with.

Johannes de silentio is trying to clarify the nature of faith. In so doing, he doubtless contributes to what Kierkegaard himself tried to achieve in his pseudonymous literature, a goal that I think is reflected in this famous comment about the pseudonymous authors:

> [T]heir importance ... unconditionally does not consist in making any new proposal, some unheard-of discovery, or in founding a new party and wanting to go further, but precisely in the opposite, in wanting to have no importance, ... in wanting, ... once again to read through solo, if possible in a more inward way, the original text of individual human existence-relationships, the old familiar text handed down from the fathers.[11]

C. Stephen Evans

---

[11] *Concluding Unscientific Postscript*, pp. 629–30.

Chronology

publishes his work, though sections are later incorporated into *Two Ethical-Religious Essays*

1847   Publishes *Upbuilding Discourses in Various Spirits* and *Works of Love*

1848   Publishes *Christian Discourses* and *The Crisis and a Crisis in the Life of an Actress*. He completes *The Point of View for My Work as an Author*, but the work is only published posthumously

1849   Publishes *The Sickness unto Death*, *Two Ethical-Religious Essays*, and two books of religious discourses: *The Lily in the Field and the Bird of the Air* and *Three Discourses at the Communion on Fridays*

1850   Publishes *Practice in Christianity* and *An Upbuilding Discourse*

1851   Publishes *Two Discourses at the Communion on Fridays*, *On My Work as an Author*, and *For Self-Examination*. *Judge for Yourself!* is written but not published until after his death

1854   Begins a public, polemical attack on the Danish Lutheran Church as a state church, first waged in *The Fatherland*, and later, in a periodical Kierkegaard himself published, *The Moment*

1855   Publishes *What Christ Judges of Official Christianity* and *The Changelessness of God*. In the midst of his controversial attack on the church, collapses on the street and dies in a hospital a few weeks later on November 11

Further reading

Three editions of Kierkegaard's collected works (*Samlede Værker*) have been produced in Denmark. The first edition (Copenhagen: Gyldendal, 1901–7) is the basis for this translation. This Danish edition is very valuable, since its pagination is included in the margins of the English language collected edition, *Kierkegaard's Writings*, edited by Howard V. Hong (Princeton: Princeton University Press, 1978–2000). The second edition of the *Samlede Værker* (Copenhagen: Gyldendal, 1920–36) is highly regarded as accurate, but is printed in a gothic font that many find difficult to read. The third edition (Copenhagen: Gyldendal, 1962–4) is the least accurate of the three, but is the basis of an electronic edition compiled by Alastair McKinnon that is available in the Past Masters series from InteLex.

Kierkegaard's surviving papers and journals were published in a multi-volume Danish edition in *Søren Kierkegaards Papirer* (Copenhagen: Gyldendal, 1968–78). Both the published writings and the journals and papers are currently being made available in a massive new edition, *Søren Kierkegaards Skrifter* (55 vols., including commentary volumes) that is expected to be completed in 2009 by Gad Publishers in Copenhagen. An electronic version of this edition will also be produced. Several selections from the journals are available in English. The most complete is *Søren Kierkegaard's Journals and Papers*, ed. and trans. Howard V. Hong and Edna H. Hong (Bloomington, Ind.: Indiana University Press, 1967–78). An electronic version of this edition is also available in the InteLex Past Masters series.

Prior to this volume, *Fear and Trembling* has been translated into English four times. The earliest, by Robert Payne (Oxford: Oxford

University Press, 1939), is a very free translation with no index. Walter Lowrie's translation, published with *The Sickness unto Death* (Princeton: Princeton University Press, 1941) contains some inaccuracies and archaisms, but was the version that introduced Kierkegaard to many English language readers. Other current versions include the *Kierkegaard's Writings* edition, ed. and trans. Howard V. Hong and Edna H. Hong (Princeton: Princeton University Press, 1983) and Alastair Hannay's translation (London, UK: Penguin, 1985).

Perhaps the best single volume introduction to Kierkegaard's life and thought is Julia Watkin's *Kierkegaard* (London: Geoffrey Chapman, 1997). A spirited attempt to engage the contemporary relevance of Kierkegaard's thought can be found in John Douglas Mullen, *Kierkegaard's Philosophy: Self-Deception and Cowardice in the Present Age* (New York: New American Library, 1988).

The secondary literature on *Fear and Trembling* in English is large, diverse, and uneven in quality. Recently, John Lippitt has published a *Guidebook to Kierkegaard and "Fear and Trembling"* (London: Routledge, 2003), which contains an extended discussion of many controversial issues in the text and a helpful (though by no means complete) bibliography. Edward Mooney has published *Knights of Faith and Resignation: Reading Kierkegaard's "Fear and Trembling"* (Albany, NY: State University of New York Press, 1991), a thoughtful study that highlights connections between the work and contemporary ethical discussions, including secular analogies to the dilemma faced by Abraham in the biblical story.

Robert Perkins has edited two excellent volumes of critical essays about *Fear and Trembling*: *Kierkegaard's "Fear and Trembling": Critical Appraisals* (University, Alabama: University of Alabama Press, 1981); and *International Kierkegaard Commentary: "Fear and Trembling" and "Repetition"* (Macon, Ga.: Mercer University Press, 1993). The latter is vol. VI in the International Kierkegaard Commentary series edited by Perkins.

From the large number of scholarly articles and book chapters devoted to *Fear and Trembling*, I will recommend just a few (in addition to the articles contained in the Perkins volumes noted above). C. Stephen Evans, " 'The Ethical' in *Fear and Trembling*", pp. 61–84 in *Kierkegaard's Ethic of Love: Divine Commands and Moral Obligations* (Oxford: Oxford University Press, 2004), expands and defends several of the claims made in the introduction to this volume. Gene Outka, "Religious and Moral Duty: Notes on *Fear and Trembling*", in Gene Outka and John P. Reeder, Jr. (eds.), *Religion and Morality* (Garden City, N.Y.: Anchor Books, 1973), is a clear-headed attempt to look at the relation between ethics and religion. Ronald Green's "Enough is Enough! *Fear and Trembling* Is Not about Ethics" (*Journal of Religious Ethics*, 21(1993), 191–209) has a title that accurately captures the article's thesis. Louis Mackey's "The View from Pisgah: A Reading of *Fear and Trembling*," in Josiah Thompson (ed.), *Kierkegaard: A Collection of Critical Essays* (Garden City, N.Y.: Doubleday, 1972), focuses on the literary dimension of the work. Finally, two articles by Philip Quinn, who would have been the editor of this volume were it not for his untimely death, should be noted: "Agamemnon and Abraham: the Tragic Dilemma of Kierkegaard's 'Knight of Faith'" (*Journal of Literature and Theology*, 4, 2(1990), 181–93); and "Moral Obligation, Religious Demand, and Practical Conflict," pp. 195–212 in Robert Audi and William Wainwright (eds.), *Rationality, Religious Belief, and Moral Commitment* (Ithaca, N.Y.: Cornell University Press, 1986). Philip Quinn did a great deal to connect the study of Kierkegaard to contemporary analytic philosophy and his voice is greatly missed.

C. Stephen Evans

Note on the translation

This translation is based on the text of *Frygt og Bæven* in the first Danish collected edition of Kierkegaard's works, *Søren Kierkegaards Samlede Værker*, I–XIV, ed. A. H. Drachmann, J. L. Heiberg and H. O. Lange (Copenhagen: Gyldendalske Boghandels Forlag, 1901–6), III, pp. 53–168. In preparing the translation and notes I have consulted previous English translations and notes by Robert Payne (London: Oxford University Press, 1939), Walter Lowrie (Princeton: Princeton University Press, [1941] 1954), Howard V. Hong and Edna H. Hong (Princeton: Princeton University Press, 1983), and Alastair Hannay (London: Penguin, 1985), as well as the text and commentary volumes in *Søren Kierkegaards Skrifter*, ed. Niels Jørgen Cappelørn, Joakim Garff, Johnny Kondrup, Alastair McKinnon, and Finn Hauberg Mortensen (Copenhagen: Søren Kierkegaard Forskningscenteret and Gads Forlag, 1997–), vol. 4, pp. 97–210, and commentary vol. K4, pp. 101–67. I am grateful to Julia Watkin (now deceased), C. Stephen Evans, Marilyn G. Piety, and Robert L. Perkins for reading the manuscript and offering helpful suggestions; to Bruce H. Kirmmse for his advice on several items of translation; to Céline Léon for checking the translations of Latin phrases in the text; and to Robert L. Perkins for assistance with the translation of German terms and passages in the text. Responsibility for the final text, however, rests solely with the translator. Thanks are due also to Susan Connell Derryberry, Supervisor of the Stetson University Library Interlibrary Loan Services, for assistance in obtaining books relating to the project, and to Cynthia Wales Lund, Special Collections Librarian at the Howard V. and Edna H. Hong Kierkegaard Library of St. Olaf College, for providing office space and access to the special collections of the library to check works cited by Kierkegaard in the text. Greek terms and passages in the text appear as they are in the first Danish collected edition, that is, generally without breathing and accent marks. Readers should note that all numbered footnotes are the translators', while the lettered footnotes are by Kierkegaard.

Sylvia Walsh

FEAR AND TREMBLING

A Dialectical Lyric
by
Johannes de silentio

What Tarquin the Proud communicated in his garden
with the beheaded poppies was understood
by the son but not by the messenger.
Hamann[1]

[1] Quoted in German from Johann Georg Hamann (1730–88), *Hamann's Schriften*, I–VIII, ed. Friedrich Roth (Berlin: Bey G. Reimer, 1821–43), III, 190. See *Katalog over Søren Kierkegaards Bibliotek* (Copenhagen: Munksgaard, 1957), nos. 536–44 (hereafter cited by the siglum KSKB followed by entry number). The son of Tarquin the Proud (?-495? BCE), seventh and last king of Rome, sent a message to his father asking how to treat the rulers of Gabii, a city with which the king was at war and where his son had contrived to become a military leader. Distrusting the messenger, the king replied by taking him to the royal garden and cutting off the heads of the tallest poppies with his cane, indicating that the son should put the leading men of Gabii to death.

Preface

Not only in the commercial world but in the realm of ideas as well, our age is holding a veritable clearance sale.[1] Everything is had so dirt cheap that it is doubtful whether in the end anyone will bid. Every speculative score-keeper who conscientiously keeps account of the momentous march of modern philosophy, every lecturer, tutor, student, every outsider and insider in philosophy does not stop at doubting everything but goes further.[2] Perhaps it would be inappropriate and untimely to ask them where they are actually going, but it is surely polite and modest to take it for granted that they have doubted everything, since otherwise it would certainly be peculiar to say that they went further. All of them then have made this preliminary movement, and presumably so easily that they do not find it necessary to drop a hint about how, for not even the one who anxiously and worriedly sought a little enlightenment found so much as an instructive tip or a little dietary prescription on how to conduct oneself under this enormous task. "But Descartes has done it, hasn't he?" Descartes,[3] a venerable, humble, honest thinker whose writings surely no one can read without the deepest emotion, has done what he has said and said what he has done. Alas! Alas! Alas! That is a

---

[1] *ein wirklicher Ausverkauf.*

[2] Probably an allusion to the Danish Hegelian philosophers, most notably Hans Lassen Martensen (1808–1884), who sought to go beyond not only previous philosophers in transcending faith as well as doubt in philosophy but also beyond their mentor, the German philosopher Georg Wilhem Friedrich Hegel (1770–1831), in speculative system building. On Kierkegaard's relation to the Danish Hegelians, see Jon Stewart, *Kierkegaard's Relations to Hegel Reconsidered* (Cambridge: Cambridge University Press, 2003), pp. 50–69, 307–10.

[3] The French philosopher René Descartes (1596–1650) is widely recognized as the father of modern European philosophy.

3

great rarity in our age! As he himself reiterates often enough, Descartes did not doubt with respect to faith. ("At the same time we should remember, as noted earlier, that the natural light is to be trusted only to the extent that it is compatible with divine revelation . . . But above all else we must impress on our memory the overriding rule that whatever God has revealed to us must be accepted as more certain than anything else. And although the light of reason may, with the utmost clarity and evidence, appear to suggest something different, we must still put our entire faith in divine authority rather than in our own judgment." *Principles of Philosophy*, I, § 28 and § 76).[4] Descartes has not yelled "Fire!" and made it a duty for everyone to doubt, for he was a quiet, solitary thinker, not a bellowing street watchman. He has modestly confessed that his method had importance only for himself and was based partly on his earlier distorted knowledge. ("My present aim, then, is not to teach the method which everyone must follow in order to direct his reason correctly, but only to reveal how I have tried to direct my own . . . But as soon as I had completed the course of study at the end of which one is normally admitted to the ranks of the learned, I completely changed my opinion. For I found myself beset by so many doubts and errors that I came to think I had gained nothing from my attempts to become educated but increasing recognition of my ignorance." *Discourse on Method*, pp. 2 and 3).[5] – What those ancient Greeks, who also surely understood a little about philosophy, assumed to be a task for a whole lifetime because proficiency in doubting is not achieved in a matter of days and weeks; what was achieved by the old veteran polemicist,[6] who had preserved the equilibrium of doubt through all specious arguments, bravely denied certainty of the senses and of thought, and incorruptibly defied the anxiety of self-love and the innuendos of sympathy – with that everyone in our age begins.

In our age nobody stops at faith but goes further. To ask where they are going would perhaps be foolhardy; however, it is surely a sign of courtesy and good breeding for me to assume that everyone has faith,

---

[4] Quoted in Latin from *Renati Des-Cartes Opera philosophica*. Editio ultima (Amsterdam: Blaviana, 1685), VIII, 23. See KSKB 473. Translation from *The Philosophical Writings of Descartes*, I–II, trans. John Cottingham, Robert Stoothoff, and Dugald Murdoch (Cambridge: Cambridge University Press, 1985), I, pp. 202–3 and 221.

[5] Ibid., II, pp. 112, 113.

[6] An ambiguous reference, probably to an early Greek skeptic such as Carneades (215–129 BCE), who distrusted the intellect as well as the senses.

since otherwise it would be peculiar to talk of going further. In those olden days it was different; then faith was a lifelong task because it was assumed that proficiency in believing is not achieved in either days or weeks. When the tried and tested oldster drew near to his end, having fought the good fight and kept the faith,[7] his heart was still young enough not to have forgotten that fear and trembling which disciplined the youth and was well-controlled by the man but is not entirely outgrown by any person – except insofar as one succeeds in going further as soon as possible. Where those venerable figures arrived, there everyone in our age begins in order to go further. ⟶ *Johannes de silentio?*

The present writer is not at all a philosopher; he has not understood the System,[8] whether it exists or whether it is finished. He already has enough for his weak head in the thought of what huge heads everyone in our age must have since everyone has such huge thoughts. Even if one were able to convert the whole content of faith into conceptual form, it does not follow that one has comprehended faith, comprehended how one entered into it or how it entered into one. The present writer is not at all a philosopher; he is, poetically and tastefully expressed,[9] a free-lancer[10] who neither writes the System nor makes *promises*[11] about the System, who neither swears by the System nor pledges himself *to* the System. He writes because for him it is a luxury that becomes all the more enjoyable and conspicuous the fewer who buy and read what he writes. He easily foresees his fate in an age when passion has been abandoned in order to serve scholarship, in an age when an author who wants readers must take care to write in such a way that his work can be conveniently skimmed through during the after-dinner nap, and take care to fashion his outer appearance in likeness to that polite garden apprentice in *The Advertiser*,[12] who with hat in hand and good references from the place

---

[7] 2 Timothy 4:7.

[8] The Hegelian philosophical system, the object of much irony, criticism, and ridicule in Kierkegaard's writings.

[9] *poetice et eleganter.*   [10] *Extra-Skriver.*

[11] Probably an allusion to the Danish Hegelian philosophers Rasmus Nielsen (1809–1884) and Johan Ludvig Heiberg (1791–1860), whose unfulfilled promises of a logical system of philosophy were satirized by Kierkegaard in his journals. See *Søren Kierkegaards Papirer*, 2nd enlarged edn., I–XVI, ed. Niels Thulstrup (Copenhagen: Gyldendal, 1968–78), V B 47.7; 49.5 (hereafter cited by the siglum SKP followed by volume, group, and entry number). See also Stewart, *Kierkegaard's Relations to Hegel Reconsidered*, pp. 384–5.

[12] An abbreviated reference to the local newspaper, *Berlingske politiske og Avertissements-Tidende*, which ran such an advertisement in 1843. See SKP IV A 88, editors' note.

where he was last employed recommends himself to an esteemed public. He foresees his fate of being totally ignored; he has a frightful presentiment that zealous criticism will put him through the mill many times. He dreads what is even more frightful, that one or another enterprising summarizer, a paragraph-gobbler (who in order to save scholarship is always willing to do to the writings of others what Trop[13] magnanimously did with *The Destruction of the Human Race* in order "to save good taste"), will cut him up into paragraphs and do it with the same inflexibility as the man who, in service to the system of punctuation, divided his discourse by counting the words so that there were exactly 50 words to a period and 35 to a semicolon. – I prostrate myself in deepest deference before every systematic snooper: "This is not the System, it does not have the least thing to do with the System. I invoke all the best upon the System and upon the Danish investors in this omnibus, for it is not likely to become a tower.[14] I wish them one and all good luck and prosperity."

Respectfully,
Johannes de silentio[15]

---

[13] A character in J. L. Heiberg's vaudeville play, *The Reviewer and the Beast*, who writes a tragedy and then tears it in two, saying: "If it costs no more to save good taste, why shouldn't we do it then?" See KSKB 1553–9: *J. L. Heibergs Samlede Skrifter. Skuespil*, I–VII (Copenhagen: J. S. Schubothes, 1833–41), III, *Recensenten og dyret*, Act I, sc. 7, p. 221.

[14] Cf. Luke 14:28–30. Also probably another "dig" at the unfinished Hegelian philosophical system.

[15] John of silence, the pseudonymous author of the text, is an imaginary figure who claims to be neither a poet nor a philosopher but nevertheless writes in a lyrical and dialectical fashion, as indicated in the subtitle of the work.

Tuning Up

There was once a man who as a child had heard that beautiful story about how God tested[1] Abraham and how he withstood the test,[2] kept the faith, and received a son a second time contrary to expectation. When the man became older, he read the same story with even greater admiration, for life had separated what had been united in the child's pious simplicity. Indeed, the older he became, the more often his thoughts turned to that story; his enthusiasm became stronger and stronger, and yet he could understand the story less and less. Finally he forgot everything else because of it; his soul had only one wish, to see Abraham, one longing, to have been a witness to that event. His desire was not to see the beautiful regions of the Far East, not the earthly splendor of the Promised Land,[3] not that god-fearing married couple whose old age God had blessed,[4] not the venerable figure of the aged patriarch, not the vigorous youth of Isaac bestowed by God – it would not have mattered to him if the same thing had taken place on a barren heath. His longing was to accompany them on the three day journey when Abraham rode with sorrow before him and Isaac by his side. His wish was to be present at the hour when Abraham lifted up his eyes and saw Mount Moriah in the distance, the hour he left the asses behind and went up the mountain alone with Isaac, for what

---

[1] *fristede*.
[2] *Fristelsen*. See Genesis 22:1–19. The Danish word *Fristelse* literally means "temptation" and is used in two senses in this text. The first corresponds to the common biblical rendering of it as a test or trial to which one is subjected by God, as in the present instance; the second connotes the ordinary meaning associated with the term, as in being attracted or lured to do something base, wrong, or unethical.
[3] See Genesis 12:1–2; 17:8.   [4] Genesis 18:1–15; 21:1–3.

engrossed him was not the artistic weave of the imagination but the shudder of the thought.

That man was not a thinker, he felt no need to go beyond faith; it seemed to him that it must be the greatest glory to be remembered as its father and an enviable lot to possess faith, even if no one knew it.

That man was not a learned exegete, he did not know Hebrew; had he known Hebrew, then perhaps he would easily have understood the story and Abraham.

I

"And God tested Abraham and said to him, take Isaac, your only son, whom you love, and go to the land of Moriah and offer him there as a burnt offering upon a mountain that I will show you."[5]

It was an early morning; Abraham rose early, had the asses saddled, and left his tent, taking Isaac with him, but Sarah looked out the window after them as they went down through the valley[6] until she could see them no more. They rode silently for three days. On the morning of the fourth day Abraham still did not say a word but lifted up his eyes and saw Mount Moriah in the distance. He left the servant boys behind and went up to the mountain alone, leading Isaac by the hand. But Abraham said to himself: "I will not conceal from Isaac where this path is taking him." He stood still and laid his hand upon Isaac's head for a blessing, and Isaac bowed to receive it. And Abraham's countenance was paternal, his gaze was gentle, his speech exhortatory. But Isaac could not understand him, his soul could not be uplifted; he embraced Abraham's knees, he pleaded at his feet, he begged for his young life, for his fair hopes, he recalled the joy in Abraham's house, he recalled the sorrow and the solitude. Then Abraham raised the boy up and walked along holding his hand, and his words were full of comfort and exhortation. But Isaac could not understand him. He climbed Mount Moriah, but Isaac understood him not. Then he turned away from Isaac a moment, but when Isaac saw Abraham's countenance again it was changed, his eyes were

---

[5] A conflated rendering of Genesis 22:1–2.

[6] Cf. Judith 10:10 in *The New Oxford Annotated Bible with the Apocrypha/Deuteronomical Books*, 3rd edn. (New York: Oxford University Press, 2001) or *The New English Bible with the Apocrypha* (New York: Oxford University Press, 1976). See also SKP 3:3822.

wild, his appearance a fright to behold. He seized Isaac by the chest, threw him to the ground, and said: "Foolish boy, do you believe that I am your father? I am an idolater. Do you believe this is God's command? No, it is my desire." Then Isaac trembled and cried out in his anguish: "God in heaven have mercy on me, God of Abraham have mercy on me; if I have no father on earth, then you be my father!" But Abraham murmured under his breath to himself: "Lord in heaven, I thank you; it is surely better for him to believe I am a monster than to lose faith in you."

When the child is to be weaned, the mother blackens her breast, for it would indeed be a shame for the breast to look delightful when the child must not have it. So the child believes that the breast has changed, but the mother is the same, her gaze is loving and tender as always. Fortunate the one who did not need more frightful measures to wean the child!

II

It was an early morning; Abraham rose early, he embraced Sarah, the bride of his old age, and Sarah kissed Isaac, who took away her disgrace,[7] who was her pride, her hope for all generations. Then they rode silently along the way, and Abraham's eyes were fastened upon the ground until the fourth day when he lifted up his eyes and saw Mount Moriah far away, but his eyes turned again towards the ground. Silently he arranged the firewood and bound Isaac, silently he drew the knife; then he saw the ram that God had chosen. He sacrificed it and went home. – – – From that day on Abraham became old; he could not forget that God had demanded this of him. Isaac flourished as before, but Abraham's eyes were darkened, he saw joy no more.

When the child has grown larger and is to be weaned, the mother covers her breast in a maidenly manner so the child no longer has a mother. Fortunate the child who did not lose its mother in some other way!

[7] Childlessness.

III

It was an early morning; Abraham rose early, he kissed Sarah, the young mother, and Sarah kissed Isaac, her delight, her joy at all times. And Abraham rode pensively along the way; he thought of Hagar and the son whom he turned out into the desert.[8] He climbed Mount Moriah, he drew the knife.

It was a quiet evening when Abraham rode out alone, and he rode to Mount Moriah. He threw himself upon his face, he begged God to forgive his sin, that he had been willing to sacrifice Isaac, that the father had forgotten his duty toward the son. More than once he rode his lonely trail but found no peace of mind. He could not comprehend that it was a sin to have been willing to sacrifice to God the best he owned, that for which he himself would gladly have laid down his life many times. And if it were a sin, if he had not loved Isaac in this way, then he could not understand how it could be forgiven, for what sin was more grievous?

When the child is to be weaned, the mother too is not without sorrow that she and the child are more and more to be parted, that the child who first lay beneath her heart yet later reposed upon her breast will not be so close any more. Thus together they mourn this brief sorrow. Fortunate the one who kept the child so close and did not need to sorrow more!

IV

It was an early morning; everything was ready for the journey in Abraham's house. He took leave of Sarah, and the faithful servant Eliezer[9] saw him out along the road until he turned back again. They rode together in harmony, Abraham and Isaac, until they came to Mount Moriah. Yet Abraham calmly and gently prepared everything for the sacrifice, but as he turned away and drew the knife, Isaac saw that Abraham's left hand was clenched in despair, that a shudder went through his body – but Abraham drew the knife.

---

[8] See Genesis 16 and 21:9–21. Hagar, an Egyptian slave-girl belonging to Sarah, bore a son to Abraham named Ishmael; both mother and son were driven into the desert at Sarah's request after the birth of Isaac.

[9] Abraham's heir prior to the birth of Isaac. See Genesis 15:1–4.

Then they returned home again and Sarah hurried to meet them, but Isaac had lost the faith. Never a word is spoken about this in the world; Isaac never spoke to any person about what he had seen, and Abraham did not suspect that anyone had seen it.

When the child is to be weaned, the mother has more solid food on hand so the child will not perish. Fortunate the one who has this stronger nourishment handy!

In these and many similar ways that man of whom we speak pondered over this event. Every time he returned home from a pilgrimage to Mount Moriah he collapsed from fatigue, clasped his hands, and said: "Surely no one was as great as Abraham. Who is able to understand him?"

[Handwritten margin notes:] religious stage

[Handwritten notes:] The man of true + complete faith is actually rare – when tested most would not go through with it.

↳ ultimate individuality

↓

Absurdity of Life; leap of faith.

A Tribute to Abraham

If there were no eternal consciousness in a human being, if underlying everything there were only a wild, fermenting force writing in dark passions that produced everything great and insignificant, if a bottomless, insatiable emptiness lurked beneath everything, what would life be then but despair? If such were the case, if there were no sacred bond that tied humankind together, if one generation after another rose like leaves in the forest,[1] if one generation succeeded another like the singing of birds in the forest, if the human race passed through the world as a ship through the sea, as the wind through the desert, a thoughtless and futile activity, if an eternal oblivion always hungrily lay in wait for its prey and there were no power strong enough to snatch it away – then how empty and hopeless life would be! But that is why it is not so, and as God created man and woman, so he fashioned the hero and the poet or orator. The latter can do nothing that the former does, he can only admire, love, and rejoice in the hero. Yet he too is happy, no less than the former, for the hero is so to speak his better nature with which he is infatuated yet delighted that it is after all not himself, that his love can be admiration. He is the guardian spirit of recollection, he can do nothing without remembering what has been done, do nothing without admiring what has been done; he takes nothing for himself but is protective of what is entrusted to him. He follows his heart's desire, but when he has found what was sought, he wanders about to every man's door with his song and

---

[1] Allusion to the *Iliad* by the Greek epic poet Homer of the early eighth century BCE. See Homer, *Iliad*, trans. Stanley Lombardo (Indianapolis/Cambridge: Hackett Publishing, 1997), 6, pp. 149–52.

speech so that everyone may admire the hero as he does, be proud of the hero as he is. This is his achievement, his humble task, his faithful service in the house of the hero. If he remains true to his love in this way, if he struggles day and night with the cunning of oblivion, which wants to trick him out of the hero, then he has fulfilled his task; he is united with the hero, who has loved him just as faithfully, for the poet is so to speak the hero's better nature, feeble like a memory, to be sure, but also glorified like a memory. Therefore no one who was great will be forgotten, and even if it takes a long time, even if a cloud of misunderstanding whisks the hero away,[2] his lover still comes, and the more time goes by, the more steadfastly he clings to him.

No! No one who was great in the world will be forgotten, but each was great in his own way, and each in proportion to the greatness of what *he loved*. For the one who loved himself became great by himself, and the one who loved other persons became great by his devotion, but the one who loved God became greater than everybody. Each will be remembered, but each became great in proportion to his *expectation*. One became great by expecting the possible, another by expecting the eternal, but the one who expected the impossible became greater than everybody. Each will be remembered, but each was great wholly in proportion to the magnitude of that with which he *struggled*. For the one who struggled with the world became great by conquering the world, and the one who struggled with himself became greater by conquering himself, but the one who struggled with God[3] became greater than everybody. Thus there was conflict in the world, man against man, one against a thousand, but the one who struggled with God was greater than everybody. Thus there was conflict on the earth: there was the one who conquered all by his power and the one who conquered God by his powerlessness. There was the one who relied on himself and gained everything, and the one who, secure in his own strength, sacrificed everything, but the one who believed in God was greater than everybody. There was the one who was great by his power, and the one who was great by his wisdom, and the one who was great by his hope, and the one who was great by his love, but

---

[2] See ibid., 3, pp. 406–9, where the hero Paris is rescued from death and carried away in a cloud by the goddess Aphrodite.

[3] See Genesis 32:22–8, where Jacob wrestles with an agent of God and prevails, whereupon his name is changed to Israel, which means "he who strives with God" or "God strives." Cf. also Hosea 12:3–4.

Abraham was greater than everybody – great by that power whose strength is powerlessness,[4] great by that wisdom whose secret is folly,[5] great by that hope whose form is madness, great by that love which is hatred of oneself.[6]

By faith Abraham emigrated from the land of his fathers and became a foreigner in the promised land.[7] He left one thing behind and took one thing with him. He left his worldly understanding behind and took faith with him; otherwise he undoubtedly would not have emigrated but surely would have thought it preposterous. By faith he was a stranger in the promised land, and there was nothing that reminded him of what was dear to him, but his soul was tempted to wistful nostalgia by the novelty of everything. And yet he was God's chosen one, in whom the Lord was well pleased![8] In fact, had he been a castaway banished from God's grace, he could have understood it better, but now it certainly seemed like a mockery of him and his faith. There was also in the world one who lived in exile from the ancestral land which he loved.[9] He is not forgotten, nor are his songs of lamentation when in sadness he sought and found what was lost. From Abraham there is no song of lament. It is human to lament, human to weep with the one who weeps, but it is greater to believe, more blessed to behold the believer.

By faith Abraham received the promise that in his seed all the generations of the world would be blessed.[10] Time passed, the possibility was there, Abraham believed; time passed, it became preposterous, Abraham believed. There was one in the world who also had an expectation.[11] Time passed, evening drew near, he was not wretched enough to have forgotten his expectation; therefore neither will he be forgotten. Then he sorrowed, and the sorrow did not cheat him as life had done, it did everything it could for him; in the sweetness of sorrow he possessed his disappointed expectation. It is human to sorrow, it is human to sorrow

---

[4] 2 Corinthians 12:9–10. [5] 1 Corinthians 3:18–19. [6] John 12:25.
[7] Hebrews 11:8–9; cf. Genesis 12:1–7; 17:8. [8] Matthew 12:18; 17:5; Isaiah 42:1.
[9] Possibly the Old Testament prophet Jeremiah (c. 640–587 BCE), who was taken to Egypt sometime after the fall of Jerusalem in 587 BCE and who according to tradition was the author of the book of Lamentations in the Old Testament; or possibly the Roman poet Ovid (Publius Ovidius Naso, 43 BCE–CE 17/18), who was banished in CE 8 by Caesar Augustus to Tomis (modern Constanza) in the Roman colony of Dacia (modern Romania) on the Black Sea, where he wrote the elegies *Tristia* and *Epistulae ex Ponto*.
[10] Genesis 12:1–2 and 17:4.
[11] Perhaps Ovid, who continually hoped to be recalled to Rome from his banishment.

with the sorrowing one, but it is greater to believe, more blessed to behold the believer. From Abraham we have no song of sorrow. He did not mournfully count the days while time passed, he did not look at Sarah with suspicious eyes as to whether she had not become old, he did not halt the movement of the sun[12] so that Sarah would not grow old and with her his expectation, he did not soothingly sing for Sarah his mournful melody. Abraham became old, Sarah became the object of ridicule in the land, and yet he was God's chosen one and heir to the promise that in his seed all the generations of the earth would be blessed. So would it not have been better, after all, if he were not God's chosen one? What does it mean to be God's chosen one? Is it to be denied one's youthful wish in youth so that it may be fulfilled with great pains in old age? But Abraham believed and held on to the promise. If Abraham had wavered, then he would have given it up. He would have said to God: "Well, perhaps it is not your will after all that it should happen, so I will give up the wish; it was my only wish, my blessedness. My soul is sincere, I harbor no hidden resentment because you denied it." He would not have been forgotten; he would have saved many by his example but still would not have become the father of faith. For it is great to give up one's wish, but it is greater to keep a firm grip on it after having given it up; it is great to lay hold of the eternal, but it is greater to stick doggedly to the temporal after having given it up. – Then came the fullness of time.[13] If Abraham had not believed, Sarah might well have died from sorrow, and Abraham, dulled by grief, would not have understood the fulfillment but only smiled at it as at a youthful dream. But Abraham believed; therefore he was young, for the one who always hopes for the best grows old, cheated by life, and the one who is always prepared for the worst grows old prematurely, but the one who believes preserves an eternal youth. So let us pay tribute to that story! For Sarah, though aged, was young enough to crave the pleasure of motherhood, and Abraham, though grey-haired, was young enough to wish to be a father. Outwardly, the wonder is that it happened in accordance with their expectation; in a deeper sense, the wonder of faith consists in Abraham and Sarah being young enough to wish and in faith's having preserved their wish and with it their youth. He accepted the fulfillment of the promise, he accepted it

---

[12] Joshua 10:12–13.   [13] Galatians 4:4.

15

in faith, and it happened according to the promise and according to faith, for Moses struck the rock with his staff but he did not believe.[14]

So there was rejoicing in Abraham's house when Sarah stood as a bride on their golden wedding anniversary.

But it was not to remain that way; Abraham was to be tried once more. He had fought with that ingenious power which invents everything, with that vigilant enemy which never dozes, with that old man who outlives everything – he had fought with time and kept the faith. Now all the frightfulness of the struggle became concentrated in one moment. "And God tested Abraham and said to him, take Isaac your only son, whom you love, go to the land of Moriah and offer him there as a burnt offering upon a mountain that I will show you."[15]

Thus everything was lost, which is even more frightful than if it had never happened! So the Lord was only mocking Abraham! Miraculously, he made the preposterous come true; now he would see it brought to nothing again. It was indeed folly, but Abraham did not laugh at it as Sarah had done when the promise was first proclaimed.[16] Everything was lost! Seventy years of faithful expectation, the brief joy over faith's fulfillment. Who is it, then, that snatches the staff from the old man? Who is it that demands he himself must break it? Who is it that makes a man's grey hairs disconsolate? Who is it that demands he himself must do it? Is there no compassion for this venerable old man, none for the innocent child? And yet Abraham was God's chosen one, and it was the Lord who put him to the test. Now everything would be lost! The glorious remembrance of posterity, the promise in Abraham's seed, was only a whim, a passing thought of the Lord's which Abraham now must obliterate. That glorious treasure[17] which was just as old as the faith in Abraham's heart and many, many years older than Isaac, the fruit of Abraham's life, dedicated by prayer, ripened in combat – the blessing on Abraham's lips, this fruit would now be plucked prematurely and be without meaning, for what meaning would it have if Isaac must be sacrificed! That sad but still blessed hour when Abraham would take leave of everything that was dear to him, when he would once again lift up his venerable head, when his countenance would become radiant like the

---

[14] Numbers 20:11–12.   [15] Cf. Genesis 22:1–2 and n. 5 in "Tuning Up."
[16] Genesis 18:10–15. Cf. Genesis 17:17.
[17] Presumably the promise given to Abraham in Genesis 12:2.

Lord's, when he would concentrate his whole soul in a blessing that was mighty enough to make Isaac blessed all his days – that hour would not come! For Abraham would indeed take leave of Isaac, but in such a way that he himself would remain behind; death would separate them, but in such a way that Isaac would become its prey. The old man would not joyfully at death lay his hand upon Isaac in blessing, but weary of life would lay a violent hand upon Isaac. And it was God who tested him. Yes, woe! Woe to the messenger who brought such news to Abraham! Who would have dared to be the emissary of such sorrow? But it was God who tested Abraham.

But Abraham believed and believed for this life. To be sure, had his faith been only for a future life, he could indeed more easily have cast everything away in order to hurry out of the world to which he did not belong. But Abraham's faith was not like that, if there be such a faith, for that is not really faith but only the remotest possibility of faith, which faintly spies its object at the edge of the horizon yet is separated from it by a yawning abyss within which despair plays its tricks. But Abraham believed precisely for this life, that he would grow old in the land, honored by the people, blessed by posterity, forever remembered in Isaac, his dearest one in life, whom he embraced with a love for which it would be only a poor expression to say that he faithfully fulfilled a father's duty to love the son, as indeed it goes in the summons: "the son whom you love."[18] Jacob had twelve sons, one of whom he loved;[19] Abraham had only one son, whom he loved.

But Abraham believed and did not doubt; he believed the preposterous. If Abraham had doubted – then he would have done something different, something great and glorious, for how could Abraham do anything else but what is great and glorious! He would have set out for Mount Moriah, he would have chopped the firewood, lit the fire, drawn the knife – he would have cried out to God: "Do not disdain this sacrifice, it is not the best I have, that I know very well, for what is an old man compared with the child of promise, but it is the best I can give you. Let Isaac never come to know it, that he may take comfort in his youth." He would have thrust the knife into his own breast. He would have been

---

[18] Genesis 22:2.
[19] See Genesis 35:23–26 and 37:3, where it is said that Jacob (Israel) loved his youngest son Joseph more than any of his other sons because Joseph was a child of his old age (like Isaac).

admired in the world, and his name would not be forgotten; but it is one thing to be admired, another to become a guiding star that rescues the anguished.

But Abraham believed. He asked nothing for himself in an attempt to move the Lord; it was only when the just penalty against Sodom and Gomorrah was issued that Abraham came forward with his appeals.[20]

We read in those sacred scriptures: "And God tested Abraham and said: 'Abraham, Abraham, where are you?'[21] But Abraham answered: 'Here am I.'" You to whom my speech is addressed, was that the case with you? When far away you saw hard times approaching, did you not say to the mountains, "cover me," and to the hills, "fall on me?"[22] Or if you were stronger, did not your feet still drag along the way, longing as it were to be back on the old paths? When a call came to you, did you answer or not – perhaps softly and in a whisper? Not so Abraham. Cheerfully, confidently, trustingly he answered in a loud voice: "Here am I." We read further: "And Abraham rose early in the morning."[23] He hurried as if going to a celebration, and early in the morning he was at the appointed place on Mount Moriah. He said nothing to Sarah, nothing to Eliezer; indeed, who could have understood him? Did not the test by its very nature require a pledge of silence from him? "He chopped the firewood, he bound Isaac, he lit the fire, he drew the knife." My listener! Many a father has thought himself deprived of every hope for the future in losing his child, which to him was the most beloved in the world, yet surely none was a child of promise in the sense that Isaac was for Abraham. Many a father has lost his child, but then it was God, the unchanging and inscrutable will of the Almighty, whose hand took it. Not so with Abraham. A harder test was in store for him, and Isaac's fate, along with the knife, lay in Abraham's hand. And he stood there, the old man with his only hope! But he did not doubt, he did not look anxiously to the right or to the left, he did not challenge heaven with his appeals. He knew it was God the Almighty who tested him, he knew it was the hardest sacrifice that could be demanded of him, but he also knew that no sacrifice was too hard when God demanded it – and he drew the knife.

[20] Genesis 18:23–33.
[21] A conflated rendering of Genesis 22:1 with Genesis 3:9, where the Lord asks this question of Adam.
[22] Hosea 10:8. Cf. Luke 23:30, which reverses the phrases. [23] Genesis 22:3.

Who strengthened Abraham's arm? Who held up his right arm so that it did not limply collapse?[24] Anyone who looks upon this scene becomes paralyzed. Who strengthened Abraham's soul, lest everything went black before his eyes so he could see neither Isaac nor the ram? Anyone who looks upon this scene goes blind. – And yet, while it is perhaps rare enough that anyone becomes paralyzed and blind, still more rarely does anyone worthily tell what happened there. We all know it – it was only a test.

If Abraham had doubted when he stood on Mount Moriah, if he had looked about in indecision, if by chance he had spotted the ram before drawing the knife, if God had permitted him to sacrifice it instead of Isaac – then he would have gone home, everything would have been the same, he would have had Sarah, he would have kept Isaac, and yet how changed! For his descent would have been an escape, his deliverance an accident, his reward disgrace, his future perhaps perdition. Then he would have testified neither to his faith nor to God's grace but to how frightful it is to go up to Mount Moriah. Then Abraham would not be forgotten, nor Mount Moriah. Yet it would not be mentioned like Ararat, where the ark landed,[25] but spoken of as a place of dismay, because it was here that Abraham doubted.

Venerable Father Abraham! When you went home from Mount Moriah, you needed no tribute to console you for what was lost, for you indeed gained everything and kept Isaac. Was it not so? The Lord never again took him from you, but you sat happily at dinner with him in your tent, as you do in the next world forever. Venerable Father Abraham! Thousands of years have elapsed since those days, but you need no latter-day lover who can snatch your memory from the power of oblivion, for every language commemorates you – and yet you reward your lover more gloriously than anyone. In the world to come you make him blissfully happy in your bosom;[26] here you captivate his eyes and heart by the wonder of your deed. Venerable Father Abraham! Second father of the human race! You who first felt and testified to that prodigious passion which disdains the frightful battle with the raging elements and the forces of creation in order to struggle with God; you who first knew that supreme passion, the holy, pure, and humble expression for

---

[24] Exodus 17:8–13.   [25] Genesis 8:4.   [26] Luke 16:22–23.

the divine madness admired by the pagans[27] – forgive the one who would speak in praise of you if he did not do it properly. He spoke humbly, as was his heart's desire; he spoke briefly, as is becoming, but he will never forget that you needed a hundred years to get a son of your old age[28] contrary to expectation, that you had to draw the knife before you kept Isaac; he will never forget that in a hundred and thirty years you got no further than faith.

---

[27] See Plato's *Phaedrus*, 244–245d, 265a–b in *Plato: Complete Works*, ed. John M. Cooper (Indianapolis/Cambridge: Hackett Publishing, 1997).
[28] Genesis 21:5.

Problems

A Preliminary Outpouring from the Heart[1]

An old adage drawn from the external and visible world says: "Only the one who works gets the bread."[2] Oddly enough, the adage does not apply in the world where it is most at home, for the external world is subject to the law of imperfection, and here it happens again and again that the one who does not work also gets the bread, and the one who sleeps gets it more abundantly than the one who works. In the external world everything belongs to the possessor; it toils slavishly under the law of indifference, and the genie of the ring obeys whoever has the ring, whether he is a Noureddin or an Aladdin,[3] and whoever has the world's treasures has them no matter how he got them. In the world of spirit it is otherwise. Here an eternal divine order prevails, here it does not rain on both the just and the unjust, here the sun does not shine on both good and evil,[4] here it holds true that only the one who works gets the bread, only the one who was in anxiety finds rest, only the one who descends into the underworld rescues the beloved,[5] only the one who draws the knife gets Isaac. The one who will not work does not get the bread but is deceived, just as the gods

---

[1] Literally "expectoration," a coughing up, spitting out, or pouring out from (Latin: *ex*) the heart or breast (*pectus*).

[2] Cf. 2 Thessalonians 3:10.

[3] Representatives of darkness and light respectively in the play *Aladdin* (based on the fairy tale "A Thousand and One Nights") by the Danish romantic poet, Adam Oehlenschläger (1779–1850). See KSKB 1597–8: *Adam Oehlenschlägers Poetiske Skrifter*, 1–11 (Copenhagen: J. H. Schubothe, 1805), 11, pp. 75–436.

[4] Cf. Matthew 5:45.

[5] Cf. the Greek myth of Orpheus, in which Orpheus goes to the underworld in search of his wife Eurydice.

deceived Orpheus with an airy apparition instead of the beloved, deceived him because he was sentimental, not courageous, deceived him because he was a lute player, not a man.[6] Here it does not help to have Abraham for a father,[7] nor seventeen noble ancestors. What was written about the maidens of Israel[8] applies to the one who will not work: he brings forth wind, but the one who is willing to work gives birth to his own father.

There is a form of knowledge that presumptuously wants to introduce into the world of spirit the same law of indifference under which the external world sighs. It thinks it is enough to know the great; other work is not needed. But that is why it gets no bread; it perishes from hunger while everything is transmuted into gold.[9] And what does it really know? There were many thousands of Greek contemporaries and countless numbers in later generations who knew all the triumphs of Miltiades,[10] but there was only one who became sleepless over them.[11] There were countless generations who knew the story of Abraham word for word by heart, but how many did it make sleepless?

Now the story of Abraham has the extrarordinary quality of always being glorious no matter how poorly it is understood, but here again it is a matter of whether one is willing to labor and be heavy laden.[12] But one does not want to work and yet wants to understand the story. One speaks in Abraham's honor, but how? By presenting the whole story in quite ordinary terms: "The great thing was that he loved God so much that he was willing to sacrifice the best to him."[13] That is very true, but "the best" is a vague term. In the course of thinking and jabbering away, one quite confidently identifies Isaac and the best, and the meditator can very

---

[6] Cf. Plato's version of the myth of Orpheus in the *Symposium*, 179d, where Orpheus is described as being "soft" or effeminate because he was a cithara or lute player who charmed his way into Hades by playing music rather than dying for the sake of love.

[7] Matthew 3:9.   [8] Isaiah 26:18.

[9] Cf. the Greek legend of King Midas, to whom the god Dionysius (Bacchus) granted the power of turning everything he touched into gold, even his food. See Ovid's account in *Tales from Ovid*, trans. Ted Hughes (New York: Farrar, Straus and Giroux, 1997), pp. 188–97.

[10] An Athenian general and statesman who defeated the Persians in the battle of Marathon in 490 BCE.

[11] Themistocles, according to Plutarch, because he sensed that the victory at Marathon was a prelude to further conflict, not the end of the war; thus he ambitiously prepared to lead the Greeks in future battles. See KSKB 1197–1200: *Plutark's Levnetsbeskrivelser*, I–IV, trans. Stephan Tetens (Copenhagen: Brummer, 1800–11), II, p. 7. In English see Plutarch, *The Rise and Fall of Athens: Nine Greek Lives*, trans. Ian Scott-Kilvert (Harmondsworth, UK: Penguin, 1960), 3.3, p. 80.

[12] Cf. Matthew 11:28.   [13] Cf. John 3:16.

well smoke his pipe while cogitating, and the listener can very well stretch out his legs comfortably. If that rich young man whom Christ met on his way[14] had sold all his possessions and given the money to the poor, we would then praise him as we do everything that is great and would not even understand him without working, but he still would not have become an Abraham even though he sacrificed "the best." What is left out of Abraham's story is the anxiety, for to money I have no ethical obligation, but to the son the father has the highest and most sacred duty. Yet anxiety is a dangerous subject for the delicate natured; therefore one forgets it, in spite of the fact that one wants to talk about Abraham. One speaks, then, and in the course of orating interchanges the two terms, "Isaac" and "the best," and everything goes splendidly. However, if it so happened that among the listeners there was a man who suffered from insomnia, then the most frightful, the most profound tragic and comic misunderstanding lies very close. He went home, he would do just like Abraham, for the son is after all "the best." If that speaker heard of it, he perhaps went to the man, gathered all his clerical dignity, and shouted: "You detestable person, you pariah of society, what devil has so possessed you that you want to murder your son?" And the parson, who had not felt any warmth or perspiration while preaching on Abraham, would be surprised at himself, at the earnest wrath with which he fulminated against that poor man. He would be pleased with himself, for never had he spoken with such force and fervor. He would say to himself and his wife: "I am an orator; what was lacking has been the occasion. When I spoke about Abraham last Sunday, I did not feel moved at all." If this same speaker had a modest excess of understanding to spare, then I think he would have lost it if the sinner calmly and in a dignified manner had replied: "After all, that was what you yourself preached on last Sunday." How could the parson even get such an idea into his head? And yet it was certainly so, and the mistake was simply that he had not known what he was saying. Yet there is no poet who could bring himself to prefer situations like this to the stuff and nonsense that fills comedies and novels! The comic and the tragic touch each other here in absolute infinity. In itself the parson's discourse was perhaps ludicrous enough but became infinitely ludicrous by its effect, and yet this was quite natural. Or suppose the sinner, without making any objection, actually

[14] Matthew 19:16–22.

became converted by the parson's castigation; suppose this zealous clergyman went cheerfully home, elated in the consciousness that he was effective not only from the pulpit but above all with his irresistible power as a spiritual advisor, inasmuch as he inspired the congregation on Sundays while on Mondays he stood like a cherub with flaming sword[15] before the one who by his action would put to shame the old saying that things do not happen in the world as the parson preaches.[a]

However, if the sinner was not convinced, then his situation is indeed tragic. He would probably be executed or sent to the madhouse; in short, he would become unhappy in relation to so-called actuality, although in another sense I certainly think that Abraham made him happy, for the one who works does not perish.

How does one explain such a contradiction as that speaker's? Is it because Abraham has a prescriptive right to be a great man, so that whatever he does is great and when another person does the same thing it is a sin, a flagrant sin? In that case I do not wish to be party to such thoughtless tribute. If faith cannot make it a holy act to be willing to murder one's son, then let the same judgment be passed upon Abraham as upon everybody else. If one perhaps lacks courage to think one's thought through to say that Abraham was a murderer, then it would certainly be better to acquire that courage than to waste time on undeserved tributes. The ethical expression for what Abraham did is that he intended to murder Isaac; the religious expression is that he intended to sacrifice Isaac. But in this contradiction lies precisely the anxiety that indeed can make a person sleepless, and yet Abraham is not who he is without this anxiety. Or perhaps Abraham did not do what is narrated there at all, perhaps due to circumstances of the time it was something entirely different; then let us forget him, for what is worthwhile in remembering the past that cannot become a present? Or perhaps that speaker had forgotten something corresponding to the ethical oversight that Isaac was the son. For if faith is taken away by becoming null and void, all that remains is the brutal fact that Abraham intended to murder

---

[a] In olden days people said: "It is sad that things do not happen in the world as the parson preaches." Perhaps the time will come, especially with the help of philosophy, when people can say: "Fortunately things do not happen as the parson preaches, for life still has a little meaning, but in his sermon there is none."

[15] Cf. Genesis 3:24.

Isaac, which is easy enough for anyone to imitate who does not have faith, that is, the faith that makes it difficult for him.

Personally, I do not lack the courage to think a thought whole. So far I have feared none, and should I encounter one like that, then I hope at least to have the honesty to say I am afraid of this thought, it stirs up something strange in me and therefore I will not think it. If I do wrong by that, then punishment certainly will not fail to come. If I had acknowledged as true the judgment that Abraham was a murderer, I do not know whether I could have silenced my reverence for him. However, if I had thought that, then I would probably have kept silent about it, for one should not initiate others into such thoughts. But Abraham is no illusion, he has not slept his way to renown, he did not owe it to a caprice of fortune.

Can one then speak candidly about Abraham without running the risk that an individual in mental confusion might go and do likewise? If I dare not, then I will keep absolutely silent about Abraham, and above all I will not scale him down in such a way that precisely by that he becomes a snare for the weak. For if one makes faith everything, that is, makes it what it is, then I certainly think one may dare speak about it without risk in our age, which is scarcely extravagant in faith, and it is only by faith that one acquires a resemblance to Abraham, not by murder. If one makes love into a fleeting sentiment, a sensual feeling in a person, then one only sets traps for the weak in wanting to talk about the exploits of love. Certainly everyone has passing emotions, but if as a result everyone wanted to perform the frightful act that love has sanctified as an immortal feat, then everything is lost, both the exploit and the one gone astray.

It is no doubt permissible, then, to speak about Abraham, for the great can never do harm when construed in its greatness; it is like a double-edged sword that kills and saves.[16] If the lot fell on me to speak about him, I would begin by showing what a devout and god-fearing man Abraham was, worthy to be called God's chosen one. Only someone like that is put to such a test, but who is such a person? Next I would describe how Abraham loved Isaac. To that end I would bid all good spirits to stand by me so that my speech would be as glowing as paternal love. I hope to describe it in such a way that not many a father in the king's realms and lands would dare to claim that he loved in this way. But

---

[16] Cf. Hebrews 4:12.

25

if he did not love as Abraham loved, then any thought of sacrificing Isaac would surely be a temptation.[17] One could already talk about this for several Sundays; certainly there is no need to hurry. If it were told properly, the result would be that some fathers would by no means insist on hearing more but for the time being would be pleased if they actually succeeded in loving as Abraham loved. If there were then one who, after having heard about the greatness but also about the frightfulness of Abraham's deed, ventured to proceed upon that trail, I would saddle my horse and ride with him. At every stop before coming to Mount Moriah I would explain to him that he could still turn back, could repent the misunderstanding that he was called to be tried in such a conflict, could acknowledge that he lacked courage, so that God himself must take Isaac if he wanted to have him. It is my conviction that such a person is not repudiated, that he can become blessed along with everyone else, but not in time. Would not such a person be judged in this way even in the times of greatest faith? I knew a person who on one occasion could have saved my life if he had been magnanimous. He said plainly: "I see well enough what I could do, but I dare not do it, I am afraid that later I will lack strength and regret it." He was not magnanimous, but who for that reason would not continue to love him?

Having spoken thus and stirred the audience so they were really sensible of the dialectical struggles of faith and its gigantic passion, then I would not be guilty of an error on the part of the audience should they think: "Well now, he has faith to such a high degree, it is already enough for us just to hold on to his coattails."[18] For I would add: "By no means do I have faith. I am by nature a clever fellow and such persons always have great difficulties in making the movement of faith, except that I certainly do not attribute in itself *any worth to the difficulty which brought the clever fellow [no] further by overcoming it than to the point where the simplest and most innocent person arrives more easily.*"

---

[17] *Anfægtelse*, which may connote either an unethical temptation (*Fristelse*), as in the present instance and throughout this text (with one exception), or a spiritual trial in the form of a scruple, hesitancy, or misgiving in relation to a command from the divine that brings the ethical into conflict with it in such a way that the ethical itself constitutes a temptation. See n. 2 of "Tuning Up" above and Kierkegaard's discussion of the distinction between temptation (*Fristelse*) and spiritual trial (*Anfægtelse*) in *Concluding Unscientific Postscript to "Philosophical Fragments,"* II, ed. and trans. Howard V. Hong and Edna H. Hong (Princeton: Princeton University Press, 1992), I, pp. 458–9.

[18] Cf. Matthew 9:20–22.

Love surely has its priests in the poets, and occasionally one hears a voice that knows how to honor it, but on faith not a word is heard. Who speaks in honor of this passion? Philosophy goes further. Theology sits by the window all made up and courts its favor, offering to sell its delights to philosophy. It is said to be difficult to understand Hegel but to understand Abraham is a small matter. To go beyond Hegel is a miracle but to manage Abraham is the easiest thing of all. I for one have devoted considerable time to understanding the Hegelian philosophy; I believe also that I have understood it fairly well, and I am foolhardy enough to think that when I cannot understand him in certain passages in spite of the effort applied, then probably he himself has not been entirely clear. All this I do easily, naturally, without getting a headache from it. However, when I must think about Abraham, I am virtually annihilated. At every moment I am aware of that prodigious paradox which is the content of Abraham's life; at every moment I am repelled, and in spite of all its passion, my thought cannot penetrate it, cannot make a hairs-breadth of headway. I strain every muscle to get a perspective, and at the same instant I become paralyzed.

I am not unacquainted with what has been admired as great and magnanimous in the world; my soul feels an affinity with it and in all humility is convinced that it was my cause too for which the hero struggled, and in a moment of meditation I cry out to myself: "Now your interest is at stake."[19] I *think* myself *into* the hero; I cannot think myself into Abraham. When I reach that height I fall down since what is offered to me is a paradox. Yet by no means do I therefore think that faith is something lowly but on the contrary that it is the highest, plus that it is dishonest of philosophy to proffer something else instead and to make light of faith. Philosophy cannot and must not bestow faith but must understand itself and know what it has to offer and take nothing away and least of all trick people out of something by making them think it is nothing. I am not unacquainted with life's hardships and dangers; I fear them not and go to meet them dauntlessly. I am not unfamiliar with the frightful; my memory is a faithful spouse and my imagination is what I myself am not, a busy little maid who sits quietly all day at her work and

---

[19] *jam tua res agitur.* Cf. Horace (Quintus Horatius Flaccus, a Latin poet of 65 BCE–CE 8), *Epistles*, I, 18, p. 84: *nam tua res agitur, paries quum proximus ardet.* See KSKB 1248: *Q. Horatii Flacci Opera* (Leipzig: Tauchnitii, 1828), p. 254; *Epistles: Book I*, ed. Roland Mayer (Cambridge: Cambridge University Press, 1994), p. 82.

in the evening knows how to chatter so prettily to me that I have to look at it even though it is not always just landscapes or flowers or idyllic pastoral scenes she paints. I have looked the frightful in the eye; I do not timidly flee from it but know very well that even if I approach it bravely my courage still is not the courage of faith and is nothing to be compared with that. I cannot make the movement of faith, I cannot shut my eyes and plunge confidently into the absurd; that is for me an impossibility, but I do not praise myself for it. I am convinced that God is love;[20] this thought has for me a primordial lyrical validity. When it is present to me I am unspeakably happy; when it is absent I long for it more intensely than the lover for the object of his love. But I do not believe; this courage I lack. To me God's love, both in a direct and inverse sense, is incommensurable with the whole of actuality. I am not cowardly enough therefore to whine and wail, but neither am I perfidious enough to deny that faith is something much higher. I can well endure living in my own fashion, I am happy and content, but my joy is not that of faith and in comparison with that is really unhappy. I do not trouble God with my petty cares; the particular does not concern me, I gaze only at my love and keep its virginal flame pure and clear. Faith is convinced that God is concerned about the least thing. I am content in this life to be wedded to the left hand. Faith is humble enough to ask for the right, for that it is humility I do not and shall never deny.

I wonder, is anyone in my age actually capable of making the movements of faith? Unless I am very much mistaken, it is rather inclined to be proud of doing what it presumably does not even believe me capable of, that is, the imperfect. It goes against the grain for me to do what so often happens, to speak inhumanly about the great as if a few millennia were an immense distance. I prefer to speak humanly about it, as if it happened yesterday, and let only the greatness itself be the distance that either exalts or condemns. If I then (*in the capacity of tragic hero*, for I cannot come higher) were summoned to such an extraordinary royal progression as the one to Mount Moriah, I know very well what I would have done. I would not have been cowardly enough to stay home, nor lagged and loafed along the road, nor forgotten the knife in order that there might be a little delay. I am fairly certain that I would have arrived there on the dot and had everything in order – more than likely I would probably have

---

[20] I John 4:8–9.

arrived too early in order to get it over with sooner. But I also know what else I would have done. The moment I mounted the horse I would have said to myself: "Now all is lost; God demands Isaac, I sacrifice him and with him all my joy – yet God is love and continues to be that for me, for in temporality God and I cannot converse, we have no language in common." Perhaps someone or other in our age would be foolish enough and envious enough of the great to want to make himself and me believe that if I had actually done this I would then have done something even greater than what Abraham did, for my immense resignation would be far more ideal and poetic than Abraham's pettiness. And yet this is the greatest falsehood, for my immense resignation would be a substitute for faith. I could not make more than the infinite movement in order to find myself and once again be in equilibrium. Nor could I have loved Isaac as Abraham loved him. That I was determined to make the movement could prove my courage, humanly speaking; that I loved him with my whole heart is a precondition without which the whole thing becomes a misdeed. But I still did not love as Abraham did, for I would have held back at the last minute, without therefore arriving too late at Mount Moriah. Furthermore, I would have spoiled the whole story by my conduct, for if I had received Isaac again, I would then have been in an awkward position. What came easiest for Abraham would have been difficult for me – once again to be joyful with Isaac! – for whoever has made the infinite movement with all the infinity of his soul, of his own accord and on his own responsibility,[21] and cannot do more only keeps Isaac with pain.

But what did Abraham do? He arrived neither too *early* nor too late. He mounted the ass and rode slowly along the way. During all this time he believed; he believed that God would not demand Isaac of him, while he still was willing to sacrifice him if it was demanded. He believed by virtue of the absurd, for human calculation was out of the question, and it was indeed absurd that God, who demanded it of him, in the next instant would revoke the demand. He climbed the mountain, and even at the moment when the knife gleamed he believed – that God would not demand Isaac. He was no doubt surprised then at the outcome, but by a double movement he had regained his original condition and therefore received Isaac more joyfully than the first time. Let us go further. We let

---

[21] *proprio motu et propriis auspiciis.*

Isaac actually be sacrificed. Abraham believed. He did not believe that he would be blessed one day in the hereafter but that he would become blissfully happy here in the world. God could give him a new Isaac, call the sacrificed one back to life. He believed by virtue of the absurd, for all human calculation had long since ceased. That sorrow can make a person mentally deranged is apparent and hard enough; that there is a willpower which can pull so drastically to windward that it rescues the understanding even though the person becomes a little peculiar is also apparent. I do not mean to disparage that, but to be able to lose one's understanding and along with it the whole of finitude, whose stockbroker it is, and then by virtue of the absurd to recover precisely this same finitude – that appalls my soul. But I do not for that reason say that it is something insignificant when on the contrary it is the only miracle. One generally thinks that what faith produces is not a work of art but a coarse and crude piece of workmanship only for the more uncultured natures, but it is far different. The dialectic of faith is the finest and most remarkable of all; it has an elevation of which I can certainly form a conception, but nothing more. I can make the great trampoline leap whereby I pass over into infinity; my spine is like a tightrope walker's, twisted from my childhood. Thus it is easy for me to go one, two, three, and turn a somersault in existence, but the next movement I cannot make, for the miraculous I cannot perform but only be amazed by it. Indeed, if at the moment Abraham swung his leg over the ass's back he had said to himself, "now Isaac is lost, I could just as well sacrifice him here at home as travel the long way to Moriah," then I do not need Abraham, whereas I now bow before his name seven times and before his deed seventy times.[22] This he has not in fact done, which I can prove by his being delighted to receive Isaac back, truly inwardly delighted, and by his needing no preparation, no time to collect himself in finitude and its joy. If that was not the case with Abraham, then he perhaps loved God but did not believe, for whoever loves God without faith considers himself, but whoever loves God with faith considers God.

Abraham stands at this point. The last stage he loses sight of is infinite resignation. He actually goes further and arrives at faith, for all those caricatures of faith – the sorry, half-hearted apathy that thinks: "Never mind, it's not worth worrying about ahead of time;" the paltry hope that

[22] Matthew 18:21–22.

says: "One can't know what will happen, it still might be possible" – those caricatures are native to the wretchedness of life and have already been infinitely disdained by infinite resignation.

Abraham I cannot understand; in a certain sense I can learn nothing from him except to be amazed. If one imagines that one may be moved to believe by pondering the outcome of that story, then one cheats oneself and wants to cheat God out of the first movement of faith; one wants to suck worldly wisdom out of the paradox. Perhaps someone or other will succeed, for our age does not stop at faith nor with its miracle of turning water into wine;[23] it goes further and turns wine into water.

Would it not be best, however, to stop at faith? And is it not shocking that everybody wants to go further? If people in our age will not abide with love, as indeed is proclaimed in various ways, what is it all coming to? To worldly shrewdness, petty calculation, to paltriness and wretchedness, to everything that can make humanity's divine origin doubtful.[24] Would it not be best to remain standing at faith, and for the one who stands to see to it that he does not fall?[25] For the movement of faith must constantly be made by virtue of the absurd, yet in such a way, mind you, that one does not lose the finite but gains it entire. For my part, I can very well describe the movements of faith, but I cannot make them. If one wants to learn how to swim, one can let oneself be suspended in a sling from the ceiling and very well go through the motions, but one is not swimming. Likewise, I can describe the movements of faith, but if I am thrown into the water, I may well swim (for I do not belong among waders), but I make different movements. I make the movements of infinity, whereas faith does the opposite; after having made the movements of infinity, it makes those of finitude. Anyone who can make these movements is fortunate; he performs the miraculous, and I shall never become tired of admiring him. It makes absolutely no difference to me whether it is Abraham or a slave in Abraham's house, a professor of philosophy or a poor servant girl, I look only at the movements. But I do pay attention to them and do not permit myself to be fooled, either by myself or by some other person. The knights of infinite resignation are easy to recognize, their gait is airy, bold. However, those who carry the treasure of faith[26] easily deceive because

---

[23] John 2:1–10.   [24] Cf. Genesis 1:27.   [25] Cf. 1 Corinthians 10:12.
[26] *Troens Klenodie*, an allusion to Bishop Hans Adolf Brorson's hymnbook, *Troens rare Klenodie* (Viborg: s. n., 1834), which Kierkegaard owned. See KSKB 199.

31

their external appearance has a striking resemblance to that which both infinite resignation and faith deeply disdain – to bourgeois philistinism.

I candidly admit that in my experience I have not found any authentic exemplar, although I do not for that reason deny that possibly every other person is such an exemplar. Nevertheless, I have sought in vain for several years to track one down. People generally travel around the world to see rivers and mountains, new stars, flamboyant birds, freakish fish, ludicrous breeds of humanity. They abandon themselves to the brutish stupor that gawks at existence and think they have seen something. This does not occupy me. However, if I knew where such a knight of faith lived, I would travel on foot to him, for this miracle concerns me absolutely. I would not leave him an instant but every minute pay attention to how he went about making the movements. I would consider myself settled for life and divide my time between watching him and practicing the maneuvers myself and thus spend all my time admiring him. As I said, I have not found such a person; nevertheless, I can very well imagine him. Here he is. The acquaintance is made, I am introduced to him. The moment I first set eyes on him, that very instant I thrust him away from me, jump back, clap my hands together, and say half aloud: "Dear me! Is this the person, is it actually him? He looks just like a tax collector." Nevertheless it really is him. I draw a little closer to him and pay attention to the slightest movement to see whether a little heterogeneous fraction of a signal from the infinite manifests itself – a glance, an air, a gesture, a sadness, a smile that betrayed the infinite in its heterogeneity with the finite. No! I examine his figure from head to foot to see if there might not be a crack through which the infinite peeped out. No! He is solid through and through. His footing? It is sturdy, belonging entirely to finitude. No dressed up citizen going out on a Sunday afternoon to Frederiksberg[27] treads the ground more solidly. He belongs entirely to the world; no bourgeois philistine could belong to it more. Nothing is detectable of that foreign and noble nature by which the knight of infinite resignation is recognized. He enjoys and takes part in everything, and whenever one sees him participating in something particular, it is carried out with a persistence that characterizes the worldly person whose heart is attached to such things. He goes about his work. To see him one would think he was a pen-pusher who had lost his soul in

---

[27] A suburb of Copenhagen containing a palace with a public park.

Italian bookkeeping,[28] so exact is he. He takes a holiday on Sundays. He goes to church. No heavenly look or any sign of the incommensurable betrays him. If one did not know him, it would be impossible to distinguish him from the rest of the crowd, for at most his hearty, vigorous hymn singing proves that he has a good pair of lungs. In the afternoon he takes a walk in the woods. He enjoys everything he sees, the throngs of people, the new omnibuses,[29] the Sound – to meet him on the beach road one would think he was a mercenary soul taking a break just to enjoy himself in this way, for he is not a poet and I have sought in vain to pick up any poetic incommensurability in him. Towards evening he goes home, his gait as undaunted as a postman's. On the way he thinks about an appetizing little dish of warm food his wife surely has for him when he comes home, for example a roast head of lamb with vegetables. If he were to meet a kindred spirit, he would continue conversing with him all the way to Østerport[30] about this dish with a passion befitting a restaurateur. As it happens, he does not have four beans,[31] and yet he firmly believes that his wife has that delectable dish for him. If she has it, to see him eat would be an enviable sight for distinguished people and an inspiring one for the common man, for his appetite is heartier than Esau's.[32] If his wife doesn't have it – oddly enough – it is all the same to him. On the way he goes past a building site and meets another man. They talk a moment together; in no time he erects a building, having at his disposal all the resources required for that purpose. The stranger leaves him thinking he was surely a capitalist, while my admired knight thinks: "Well, if it came to that, I could easily get it." He lounges by an open window and surveys the square where he lives. Everything that happens – a rat scurrying under a gutter plank, children playing – everything engages him with a composure in existence as if he were a girl of sixteen. And yet he is no genius, for I have sought in vain to spy out the incommensurability of genius in him. He smokes his pipe in the evening; to see him one would swear it was the local tradesman across the way vegetating in the twilight. He lets things take their course

---

[28] Double entry bookkeeping (double posting as a debit and a credit) was introduced in 1504 by the Italian monk, Boccaccio da Borgo.
[29] Horse-drawn omnibuses or coaches capable of carrying many passengers were introduced in Copenhagen in 1840.
[30] A gate to the city.
[31] A Danish colloquial expression referring to the *skilling*, an obselete coin worth about a British farthing or half a cent in US currency.
[32] Genesis 25:29–34.

with a freedom from care as if he were a reckless good-for-nothing and yet buys every moment he lives at the opportune time for the dearest price, for he does not do even the slightest thing except by virtue of the absurd. And yet, yet – yes, I could fly into a rage over it, if for no other reason than out of envy – yet this person has made and at every moment is making the movement of infinity. He empties the deep sadness of existence in infinite resignation, he knows the blessedness of infinity, he has felt the pain of renouncing everything, the dearest thing he has in the world, and yet the finite tastes every bit as good to him as to someone who never knew anything higher, for his remaining in finitude has no trace of a dispirited, anxious training, and yet he has this confidence to delight in it as if it were the most certain thing of all. And yet, yet the whole earthly figure he presents is a new creation[33] by virtue of the absurd. He resigned everything infinitely and then grasped everything again by virtue of the absurd. He constantly makes the movement of infinity, but he does it with such precision and proficiency that he constantly gets finitude out of it and at no second does one suspect anything else. It is supposed to be the most difficult task for a dancer to leap into a particular posture in such a way that there is no second when he grasps at the position but assumes it in the leap itself. Perhaps no dancer can do it – but that knight does. The majority of people live absorbed in worldly sorrow and joy; they are wallflowers who do not join in the dance. The knights of infinity are dancers and have elevation. They make the upward movement and drop down again, and this too is not an unhappy pastime nor unlovely to behold. But every time they drop down they cannot assume the posture at once; they hesitate an instant, and this hesitation shows that they are really strangers in the world. This is more or less conspicuous in proportion to their artistry, but even the most skillful of these knights still cannot hide this hesitation. One does not need to see them in the air but only at the instant they touch and have made contact with the ground to recognize them. But to be able to land in such a way that it looks as if one were simultaneously standing and walking, to transform the leap of life into a gait, absolutely to express the sublime in the pedestrian – that only the knight of faith can do – and that is the only miracle.

However, this miracle can so easily deceive that I shall therefore describe the movements in a particular instance which may illuminate their relation to actuality, for everything revolves around that. A youth

---

[33] 2 Corinthians 5:17.

34

falls in love with a princess and the whole content of his life consists in this love, and yet the relation is such that it cannot possibly be realized, cannot possibly be translated from ideality into reality.[b] The slaves of misery, the frogs in the swamp of life, naturally screech: "Such a love is foolishness; the rich brewer's widow is just as good and sound a match." Let them croak in the swamp undisturbed. The knight of infinite resignation does not act like that, he does not give up the love, not for all the world's glory. He is no fool. He first makes sure that it really is the content of his life, and his soul is too healthy and too proud to waste the least thing on an intoxication. He is not cowardly, he is not afraid to let it steal into his most secret, his most remote thoughts, to let it wind in countless coils around every ligament in his consciousness – if the love becomes unhappy, he will never be able to wrench himself out of it. He feels a blissful sensual pleasure in letting love palpitate through every nerve, and yet his soul is as solemn as that of one who has drained the cup of poison[34] and feels how the juice penetrates every drop of blood – for this moment is one of life and death. Having thus imbibed all the love and immersed himself in it, he then does not lack the courage to attempt and risk everything. He surveys the circumstances of life and gathers the rapid thoughts which like well-trained doves obey his every signal; he waves a wand over them and they scurry in all directions. But when they now all return as messengers of sorrow and explain to him that it is an impossibility, he becomes quiet, dismisses them, remains alone, and then undertakes the movement. If what I say here is to have any significance, it is essential that the movement be carried out properly.[c] In the first place,

---

[b] It goes without saying that whatever other interest in which an individual has concentrated the whole reality of actuality can, if it proves unrealizable, give rise to the movement of resignation. However, I have chosen a love affair to illustrate the movements because this interest no doubt will be more readily understood and thus relieves me of all preliminary considerations that in a deeper sense could only be of concern to very few individuals.

[c] *For that passion is required. Every movement of infinity occurs through passion, and no reflection can bring about a movement. This is the perpetual leap in existence that explains the movement, whereas mediation is a chimera which according to Hegel is supposed to explain everything and which is also the only thing he has never tried to explain.*[35] Even to make the well-known Socratic distinction between what one understands and what one does not understand requires passion, and naturally still more to make the genuinely Socratic movement of ignorance.[36] What our age lacks is not reflection but passion. In a certain sense, therefore, the age is really too tenacious of life to die, for dying is one of the most remarkable leaps. A little verse by a poet has always appealed to me a great deal because, after beautifully and simply having wished good things in life for himself in five or six previous lines, he ends like this: "a blessed leap into eternity."[37]

[34] Probably an allusion to the Athenian philosopher Socrates (c. 469–399 BCE), whose death by drinking hemlock is recounted in Plato's *Phaedo*.

35

the knight will then have strength to concentrate the whole content of life and the meaning of actuality into one single wish. If a person lacks this concentration, this focus, if his soul is dispersed in the manifold from the beginning, then he never comes to make the movement. He will act shrewdly in life like those financiers who invest their capital in all sorts of securities in order to gain on the one when they lose on the other – in short, then, he is not a knight. Next, the knight will have strength to concentrate the result of all his reflection into one act of consciousness. If he lacks this focus, if his soul is dispersed in the manifold from the beginning, then he will never have time to make the movement; he will constantly be running errands in life, never entering eternity, for even at the moment when he is closest to it he will suddenly discover that he has forgotten something and consequently must go back. At the next moment he will think it is possible, and that is also quite true, but through such considerations one never comes to make the movement but by their aid sinks deeper and deeper into the mire.

The knight makes the movement, then, but which one? Will he forget the whole thing? For in that too there is certainly a kind of concentration. No! For the knight does not contradict himself, and it is a contradiction to forget the whole content of his life and yet remain the same. He feels no inclination to become another person and by no means regards that as something great. Only the lower natures forget themselves and become something new. For instance, the butterfly has entirely forgotten that it was a caterpillar; perhaps in turn it can forget that it was a butterfly so completely that it can become a fish. The deeper natures never forget themselves and never become anything other than what they were. The knight, then, will remember everything; but this recollection is precisely the pain, and yet in the infinite resignation he is reconciled with existence. The love for that princess became for him the expression of an eternal love, assumed a religious character, was transfigured into a love of the eternal being, which to be sure denied the fulfillment of the love but

---

[35] Mediation (*Vermittlung*), the reconciliation of opposing concepts in a higher unity, was a central concept in Hegel's speculative system of philosophy. See, for example, G. W. F. Hegel, *The Encyclopaedia Logic (with the Zusätze)*, trans. T. F. Geraets, W. A. Suchtung, and H. S. Harris (Indianapolis/Cambridge: Hackett Publishing, 1991), 30–31 (§§6–7); 306–7 (§§240–2).

[36] On Socratic ignorance, see Plato's *Apology*, 21a–d, 23a–b.

[37] *ein seliger Sprung in die Ewigkeit*. Source unidentified.

still reconciled him once again in the eternal consciousness of its validity in an eternal form that no actuality can take from him. Fools and young people chatter about everything being possible for a human being. However, that is a great misapprehension. Spiritually speaking, everything is possible, but in the finite world there is much that is not possible. The knight nevertheless makes this impossibility possible by expressing it spiritually, but he expresses it spiritually by renouncing it. The wish that would carry him out into actuality but came to grief over the impossibility is now turned inward but is not therefore lost or forgotten. Sometimes it is the obscure currents of desire in him that awaken the recollection; sometimes he awakens it himself, for he is too proud to be willing for the whole content of his life to have been a fleeting affair of the moment. He keeps this love young, and it increases along with him in age and beauty. However, he needs no finite occasion for its growth. From the moment he has made the movement the princess is lost. He does not need those erotic palpitations of the nerves from seeing the beloved etc., nor in a finite sense does he constantly need to take leave of her, because he recollects her in an eternal sense, and he knows very well that the lovers who are so eager to see each other once more before parting for the last time are right in being eager, right in thinking that it is the last time, for they forget each other as soon as possible. He has grasped the deep secret that even in loving another person one must be self-sufficient. He pays no further finite attention to what the princess does, and precisely this proves that he has made the movement infinitely. Here one has occasion to see whether the movement in the individual is real or simulated. There was one who also believed that he had made the movement, but lo, time passed, the princess did something else, she married a prince for example; then his soul lost the resilience of resignation. He showed thereby that he had not made the movement correctly, for whoever has resigned infinitely is self-sufficient. The knight does not cancel his resignation, he keeps his love just as young as it was in the first moment; he never lets it get away from him, precisely because he has made the movement infinitely. What the princess does cannot disturb him; it is only the lower natures that have the law governing their actions in another person, the premises for their actions outside of themselves. However, if the princess is like-minded, then something beautiful will result. She will then introduce herself to the order of knighthood into which one is not admitted by ballot but of which everyone is a member who has courage to enroll, the order of knighthood which thereby proves its immortality by making no distinction between man and woman. She too will keep her love young and sound, she too will have overcome her agony, even though she does not, as it says in the ballad, "lie by her lord's side every night."[38] These two will then be suited to each other for all eternity, with such a rhythmical, pre-established harmony[39] that if ever the moment came – a moment that nevertheless does not concern them finitely, for then they would grow old – if ever the moment came that allowed the love to be given expression in time, then they would be able to begin precisely where they would have begun if they had been united originally. Whoever understands this, whether a man or a woman, can never be deceived, for it is only the lower natures that imagine they are deceived. No girl who lacks such pride really understands what it is to love, but if she is so proud, then all the world's cunning and ingenuity cannot deceive her.

In infinite resignation there is peace and rest; every person who wills it, who has not debased himself by belittling himself, which is even more terrible than being too proud, can discipline himself to make this movement, which in its pain reconciles one with existence. Infinite resignation is that shirt mentioned in an old legend.[40] The thread is spun with tears, bleached by tears; the shirt is sewn in tears, but then it also protects better than iron and steel. The defect in the legend is that a third party can make this linen. The secret in life is that each must sew it himself, and the remarkable thing is that a man can sew it quite as well as a woman. In infinite resignation there is peace and rest and consolation in the pain, that is, when the movement is made properly. Nevertheless, it would not be difficult for me to write a whole book if I were to go through all the various misunderstandings, the awkward postures, the slipshod movements I have encountered just in my modest practice. People believe very little in spirit, and yet spirit is precisely what is needed in order to make this movement. It is essential that it not be a one-sided result of a cruel

---

[38] A paraphrase of a line from a Danish medieval folksong. See KSKB 1477–81: *Udvalgte danske Viser fra Middelalderen*, I–V, ed. W. H. F. Abrahamson et al. (Copenhagen: J. F. Schultz, 1812–14), I, p. 301.

[39] *harmonia præstabilita*. The notion of a pre-established harmony was a fundamental concept in the philosophy of the German philosopher Gottfried Wilhelm Leibniz (1646–1716).

[40] "Erzsi die Spinnerin" in Johann Grafen Mailáth, *Magyarische Sagen, Mährchen und Erzählungen*, I–II (Stuttgart and Tübingen: J. G. Cotta, 1837), II, p. 18. See KSKB 1411.

necessity,[41] and certainly the more this is granted, the more dubious it always becomes whether the movement is proper. Thus, if one thinks that a cold, barren necessity necessarily must be granted, one implies thereby that no one can experience death before actually dying, which strikes me as a crass materialism. Yet in our age people are less concerned about making pure movements. If someone who wanted to learn to dance were to say, "for centuries now one generation after another has learned the positions; it is high time for me to profit by it and without further ado begin with quadrilles," then people would no doubt laugh at him a little, but in the world of spirit it is highly plausible. What then is education? I thought it was the curriculum the individual runs through in order to catch up with himself, and whoever will not go through this curriculum is helped very little by being born in the most enlightened age.

Infinite resignation is the last stage before faith, so that whoever has not made this movement does not have faith. For only in infinite resignation do I become transparent to myself in my eternal validity, and only then can there be talk of laying hold of existence by virtue of faith.

We shall now let the knight of faith appear in the incident previously mentioned. He does exactly the same as the other knight, he infinitely renounces the love that is the content of his life and is reconciled in pain. But then the miracle occurs. He makes yet another movement more wonderful than anything, for he says: "I nevertheless believe that I shall get her, namely by virtue of the absurd, by virtue of the fact that for God everything is possible."[42] The absurd does not belong to the distinctions that lie within the proper compass of the understanding. It is not identical with the improbable, the unforeseen, the unexpected. The moment the knight resigned he assured himself of the impossibility, humanly speaking, that was the conclusion of the understanding, and he had energy enough to think it. In an infinite sense, however, it was possible by resigning it, but this possessing [of possibility], you see, is also a relinquishing [of it]; yet this possessing is no absurdity to the understanding, for the understanding continued to be right in maintaining that in the world of finitude where it rules it was and remained an

---

[41] *dira Necessitas*. See Horace, *Odes*, III, 24, 6. *Q. Horatii Flacci opera*, p. 94. In English see *The Complete Odes and Epodes*, trans. W. G. Shepherd (Harmondsworth, UK: Penguin, 1983), p. 155.
[42] Matthew 19:26. Cf. also Genesis 18:14.

impossibility. The knight of faith is clearly conscious of this as well; consequently, the only thing that can save him is the absurd, and this he lays hold of by faith. He therefore acknowledges the impossibility and at the same moment believes the absurd, for if he imagines himself to have faith without acknowledging the impossibility with all the passion of his soul and with his whole heart, then he deceives himself and his testimony is neither here nor there since he has not even attained infinite resignation.

Faith is therefore no esthetic emotion but something much higher, precisely because it presupposes resignation; it is not a spontaneous inclination of the heart but the paradox of existence. For instance, if a young girl in spite of all difficulties is still convinced that her wish will be fulfilled, this conviction is not at all that of faith, even though she is brought up by Christian parents and perhaps has gone to [confirmation classes with] the parson for a whole year. She is convinced in all her childlike naiveté and innocence, and this conviction ennobles her being and bestows upon her a supernatural magnitude, so that like a wonder worker she can conjure up the finite powers of existence and even cause stones to weep,[43] while on the other hand in her agitation she can just as well run to Herod as to Pilate[44] and move the whole world with her pleas. Her conviction is very lovely, and one can learn much from her, but one thing that cannot be learned from her is how to make movements, for her conviction dares not look the impossibility in the eye in the pain of resignation.

I can perceive, then, that it takes strength and energy and spiritual freedom to make the infinite movement of resignation. I can also perceive that it can be done. The next movement amazes me; my brain whirls in my head, for after having made the movement of resignation, now by virtue of the absurd to get everything, to get the wish, whole, unabridged – that is beyond human powers, that is a miracle. But this I can perceive, that the young girl's conviction is mere folly in comparison with the firmness of faith even though it has perceived the impossibility. Every time I want to make this movement everything goes black before my eyes

---

[43] See Ovid's *Metamorphoses*, in which the mythical musician Orpheus causes stones, trees, flowers, etc. to weep by his singing and playing. In English see *Ovid's Metamorphoses*, trans. John Dryden et al. (New York: The Heritage Press, 1961), pp. 315–19. See also KSKB 1265: *P. Ovidii Nasonis. Opera quae supersunt. Opera omnia*, ed. A. Richter (Leipzig: Vogel, 1828).

[44] Cf. Luke 23:1–25.

at the very moment I am admiring it absolutely, and at the same moment a monstrous anxiety grips my soul, for what does it mean to tempt God? And yet this is the movement of faith and remains that, even though philosophy, in order to confuse the issue, wants to make us believe that it has faith, and even though theology wants to sell it off at a cheap price.

The act of resigning does not require faith, for what I gain in resignation is my eternal consciousness, and that is a purely philosophical movement which I take comfort in making when required and which I can discipline myself to do. For whenever something finite gets beyond my control, I starve myself until I make the movement, for my eternal consciousness is my love for God, and for me that is higher than anything. The act of resigning does not require faith, but to get the least bit more than my eternal consciousness does require faith, for this is the paradox. The movements are often confused. It is said that faith is needed in order to renounce everything; indeed, one hears what is even more peculiar, that a person complains that he has lost faith and when one consults the scale to see where he is, oddly enough he has only come to the point where he should make the infinite movement of resignation. By resignation I renounce everything; this movement I make by myself, and if I do not make it, then it is because I am cowardly and soft and without enthusiasm and do not feel the importance of the higher dignity every human being is accorded to be his own censor, which is much more distinguished than being Censor General for the whole Roman republic.[45] This movement I make by myself, and what I gain as a result is myself in my eternal consciousness in blessed harmony with my love for the eternal being. By faith I do not renounce anything; on the contrary, by faith I receive everything, exactly in the sense in which it is said that one who has faith like a mustard seed can move mountains.[46] A purely human courage is required to renounce the whole of temporality in order to gain the eternal, but this I gain and never in all eternity can renounce without self-contradiction. But it takes a paradoxical and humble courage next to grasp the whole of temporality by virtue of the absurd, and this is the courage of faith. By faith Abraham did not renounce Isaac, but by faith Abraham received Isaac. By virtue of resignation that rich young

---

[45] Roman censors were magistrates appointed to take the census and to supervise public morality.
[46] Matthew 17:20.

man[47] should have given away everything, but when he had done that, the knight of faith would then have said to him: "By virtue of the absurd you will get every cent back again, if you can believe that." And the formerly rich young man should by no means be indifferent to these words, for in the event he gave away his goods because he was bored with them, his resignation would be good for nothing.

Temporality, finitude is what it is all about. I can resign everything by my own strength and then find peace and rest in the pain. I can tolerate everything; even if that awful demon more frightful than Death the King of Terrors that scares people,[48] even if madness held up a fool's costume before my eyes and I understood by its look that it was I who should put it on, I can still save my soul if I am otherwise more anxious that my love for God rather than my worldly happiness triumphs in me. Even at the last moment a person can concentrate his whole soul into one single glance toward that heaven from which all good gifts come,[49] and this glance will be understood by him and by the one whom it seeks to mean that he still remained true to his love. Then he will calmly put on the costume. Anyone whose soul lacks this romanticism has sold his soul, whether he got a kingdom or a paltry piece of silver[50] for it. But by my own strength I cannot get the least bit of what belongs to finitude, for I continually use my strength to resign everything. By my own strength I can give up the princess, and I shall not become a sulker but find joy and peace and rest in my pain. But by my own strength I cannot get her back again, for I use all my strength just for the act of resigning. But by faith, says that miraculous knight, by faith you will get her by virtue of the absurd.

Alas, this movement I cannot make. As soon as I want to begin on it, everything turns around and I fly back to the pain of resignation. I can swim in life, but for this mystical floating I am too heavy. To exist in such a way that my opposition to existence expresses itself at every moment as the most beautiful and most secure harmony with it – that I cannot do. And yet it must be glorious to get the princess. I say this every moment, and the knight of resignation who does not say it is a deceiver, he has not

[47] Luke 18:18–27; Mark 10:17–22; Matthew 19:16–22.
[48] The figure of death personified as a dancing skeleton is depicted in T. L. Borup, *Det menneskelige Livs Flugt, eller Døde-Dands* [The Flight of Human life or The Dance of Death], 3rd edn. (Copenhagen: J. H. Schubothe, 1814). See KSKB 1466.
[49] James 1:17.   [50] Cf. Matthew 26:15.

had a single wish, and he has not kept the wish young in his pain. Perhaps there was someone who found it sufficiently convenient that the wish was no longer alive, that the arrow of pain was blunted, but such a person was no knight. A freeborn soul who caught himself in that would despise himself and begin afresh and above all would not allow his soul to be self-deceived. And yet it must be glorious to get the princess; and yet the knight of faith is the only happy person and heir to the finite, while the knight of resignation is a stranger and foreigner. To get the princess in this way, to live joyfully and happily day in and day out with her (for it is also conceivable that the knight of resignation could get the princess but his soul had clearly perceived the impossibility of their future happiness), so as to live joyfully and happily every moment by virtue of the absurd, every moment to see the sword hanging over the beloved's head[51] and yet to find, not rest in the pain of resignation, but joy by virtue of the absurd – that is miraculous. The one who does that is great, the only great person. The thought of it touches my soul, which was never sparing in admiring greatness.

Now if everyone in my generation unwilling to stop at faith is actually a man who has grasped the horror of life, who has understood what Daub meant when he said that a soldier standing alone at his post with a loaded rifle by a powder magazine on a stormy night gets strange thoughts;[52] if everyone unwilling to stop at faith is actually a man who has strength of soul to grasp the thought that the wish was an impossibility and there-upon gave himself time to become solitary with it; if everyone unwilling to stop at faith is a man who is reconciled in pain and reconciled by pain; if everyone unwilling to stop at faith is a man who subsequently (and if he has not done all the foregoing, then he should not trouble himself when there is talk of faith) performed the miraculous and grasped the whole of existence by virtue of the absurd – then what I write is the highest tribute to the present generation by its lowliest member, who can make only the

---

[51] An allusion to the legendary figure Damocles, an envious courtier over whose head a sword was suspended by a hair at a banquet hosted by Dionysius, ruler of Syracuse, to illustrate the danger associated with greatness.

[52] Karl Daub (1765–1836) was a right-wing Hegelian whose remark paraphrased by Kierkegaard here is recorded in Karl Rosenkranz, *Erinnerungen an Karl Daub* (Berlin: Verlag von Duncker und Humblot, 1837), p. 24. See KSKB 743 and *Søren Kierkegaard's Journals and Papers*, I–VII, ed. Howard V. Hong and Edna H. Hong (Bloomington and London: Indiana University Press, 1967–78), I, entry no. 899 (SKP IV A 92), hereafter referred to by the siglum JP followed by volume and entry number.

movement of resignation. But why are they unwilling to stop at faith? Why does one sometimes hear that people are ashamed to acknowledge that they have faith? I cannot understand it. If I ever manage to be able to make this movement, I shall drive with four horses in the future.

Is it really so? Is all the bourgeois philistinism I see in life and which I do not permit my words but rather my works to judge, is it really not what it seems? Is it the miracle? It is indeed conceivable, for that hero of faith did indeed have a striking resemblance to it and was not even an ironist and humorist but something still higher. Much is said in our time about irony and humor, especially by people who have never known how to practice them but nevertheless know how to explain everything. I am not entirely unfamiliar with these two passions; I know a little more about them than what is said in German and German-Danish compendia. I know therefore that these two passions are essentially different from the passion of faith. Irony and humor also consider themselves and therefore belong to the sphere of infinite resignation; their flexibility is due to the fact that the individual is incommensurable with actuality.

The last movement, the paradoxical movement of faith, I cannot make, be it a duty or whatever, although there is nothing I would rather do. Whether a person has a right to say this must be left up to him; whether he can come to an amicable agreement in this respect is a matter between him and the eternal being that is the object of faith. What every person can do is to make the movement of infinite resignation, and I for my part would not hesitate to call anyone a coward who imagines that he cannot do it. With faith it is another matter. But what every person does not have a right to do is to make others believe that faith is something lowly or that it is an easy matter, whereas it is the greatest and the hardest.

People construe the story of Abraham in another way. They praise God's grace for giving Isaac to him again; the whole affair was only a trial. A trial – this word can mean much and little, and yet the whole affair is over as soon as it is said. One mounts a winged horse;[53] at that very moment one is on Mount Moriah, at that very moment one sees the ram. One forgets that Abraham only rode upon an ass, which goes slowly along

---

[53] In Greek mythology Pegasus was a winged horse that sprang from the body of Medusa upon her death and was associated with poetic inspiration inasmuch as the stamp of his hoof caused Hippocrene, the sacred fountain of the Muses (the nine goddesses who presided over literature and the arts and sciences), to be opened up on Mount Helicon.

the way, that he had a three-day journey, that he needed some time to chop the firewood, bind Isaac, and draw the knife.

And yet one pays tribute to Abraham. The speaker can just as well sleep until the last fifteen minutes before he has to speak; the listener can just as well fall asleep during the speech, for everything goes easy enough without trouble from either side. If a man who suffered from insomnia were present, he would perhaps have gone home, sat down in a corner, and thought: "The whole affair is a momentary matter; just wait a minute, then you will see the ram and the trial is over." If the speaker were to meet him in this situation, then I imagine he would step up to him in all his dignity and say: "You wretch, to let your soul sink into such folly! No miracle takes place, and the whole of life is a trial." As the speaker progressed in his effusiveness, the more excited he became and the more he was pleased with himself, and while he had noticed no congestion of blood when he talked about Abraham, he now could feel the vein swelling in his forehead. Perhaps he would be dumbfounded if the sinner calmly and with dignity replied: "Well, that was what you preached about last Sunday."

Let us then either forget Abraham or else learn to be horrified by the prodigious paradox that is the meaning of his life, so that we may understand that our age, like every age, can be joyful if it has faith. If Abraham is not a cipher, a phantom, some showpiece one uses to amuse oneself, then the fault can never lie in the sinner wanting to do likewise. But the point is to see how great what Abraham did was, so that the man can judge for himself whether he has the vocation and courage to be tried in something like this. The comic contradiction in the speaker's behavior was that he made Abraham into a nobody and yet wanted to forbid the other to conduct himself in the same way.

Should one then not dare to speak about Abraham? I think one probably should after all. If I were to speak about him, I would first depict the pain of the trial. To that end I would, like a leech, suck all the anxiety and distress and torment out of a father's suffering in order to be able to describe what Abraham suffered while still believing through it all. I would recall that the journey lasted three days and a good part of the fourth; indeed, these three and a half days must be infinitely longer than the couple of thousand years that separate me from Abraham. Then I would recall that, in my view, every person may still venture to turn back before beginning something like this and every moment can turn back repentantly. If one does this, then I fear no danger, nor am I afraid of arousing a desire in people to be tried in likeness to Abraham. But to peddle a cheap edition of Abraham and yet forbid everyone to do likewise is ludicrous.

It is now my intention to draw out in the form of problems the dialectical factors implicit in the story of Abraham in order to see what a prodigious paradox faith is – a paradox that is capable of making a murder into a holy act well pleasing to God, a paradox that gives Isaac back again to Abraham, which no thought can lay hold of because faith begins precisely where thinking leaves off.

Problem I: Is there a teleological suspension of the ethical?

The ethical as such is the universal,[54] and as the universal it applies to everyone, which may be expressed from another angle by saying that it is in force at every moment. It rests immanently in itself, has nothing outside itself that is its telos,[55] but is itself the telos for everything outside itself, and when the ethical has assimilated this into itself it goes no further. Defined immediately as a sensuous and psychical being, the single individual[56] is the particular[57] that has its telos in the universal, and it is his ethical task constantly to express himself in this, to annul his particularity in order to become the universal. As soon as the single individual wants to assert himself in his particularity over against the universal, he sins and only by acknowledging this can be reconciled again with the universal. Whenever the single individual feels an urge to assert himself as the particular after having entered into the universal, he is in a state of temptation, from which he can extricate himself only by

---

[54] See G. W. F. Hegel, *Elements of the Philosophy of Right*, ed. Allen W. Wood and trans. H. B. Nisbet (Cambridge: Cambridge University Press, 1991), pp. 195–6, §152. Kierkegaard used the second German edition of this work in *Georg Wilhelm Friedrich Hegel's Werke. Vollständige Ausgabe durch einen Verein*, I–XVIII, ed. Philipp Marheineke et al. (Berlin: Duncker und Humblot, 1832–45), VIII, p. 218. See KSKB 549–65. Kierkegaard may also have in mind the ethics of Immanuel Kant (1724–1804) as set forth, for example, in *Groundwork of the Metaphysics of Morals*, trans. Mary Gregor (Cambridge: Cambridge University Press, 1998). See Ronald M. Green, *Kierkegaard and Kant: The Hidden Debt* (Albany, N.Y.: State University of New York, 1992).

[55] τελος, meaning end, goal, or purpose.   [56] *den Enkelte*.

[57] *den Enkelte*. This term can mean "the single individual," as in the previous reference, or "the particular," the latter referring to anything that is distinct or separate in contrast to the universal, which includes all particulars or the whole. Generally the first meaning of the term predominates in this text, but in a few instances, as in the present case, the second meaning is appropriate for indicating the contrast between the particular and the universal being presented in the text.

repentantly surrendering himself as the particular to the universal. If this is the highest thing that can be said about a human being and his existence, then the ethical has the same character as a person's eternal salvation, which eternally and at every moment is his telos, since it would be a contradiction to say that could be surrendered (i.e. teleologically suspended), for as soon as that is suspended it is forfeited, whereas whatever is suspended is not forfeited but on the contrary is preserved in the higher, which is its telos.

If that is the case, then Hegel is right when in "The Good and the Conscience"[58] he lets the human being be qualified only as the particular, and he is right in regarding this qualification as a "moral form of evil" (see especially *The Philosophy of Right*) which must be annulled[59] in the teleology of the moral[60] in such a way that the single individual who remains in that stage either sins or stands in temptation. However, Hegel is wrong in speaking about faith,[61] wrong in not protesting loudly and clearly against Abraham enjoying honor and glory as a father of faith, whereas he ought to have been remanded and exposed as a murderer.

Faith is exactly this paradox, that the single individual is higher than the universal, but in such a way, mind you, that the movement is repeated, so that after having been in the universal he now as the particular keeps to himself as higher than the universal. If this is not faith, then Abraham is lost and faith has never existed in the world precisely because it has always existed. For if the ethical, i.e. the ethical life,[62] is the highest and nothing incommensurable remains in a human being in any way other than that incommensurability constituting evil, i.e. the particular that must be expressed in the universal, then one needs no other categories than what the Greek philosophers had or what can be

---

[58] *Philosophy of Right*, 157–86, §§129–41.

[59] *ophæves*. Unlike the Danish word *ophæve*, which means simply to abolish or to annul, the German term to which it refers here, *aufheben* (to sublate or suspend), is ambiguous in that it means both "to cancel" and "to preserve" in a higher unity. See Hegel, *The Encyclopedia Logic*, pp. xxv–xxvi, xxxv–xxxvi, 154, §96. See also Kierkegaard's discussion of this term in *Concluding Unscientific Postscript*, I, pp. 222–3.

[60] *det Sædeliges Teleologi*.

[61] See, for example, *Philosophy of Right*, 290–304, §270; *Phenomenology of Spirit*, trans. A. V. Miller (Oxford: Clarendon Press, 1977), pp. 321–8, §§527–37.

[62] *det Sædelige*. This term can mean the moral, as in the previous paragraph, or the ethical, as in the present context, where it is equivalent to the German term *die Sittlichkeit*, Hegel's expression for the ethical life in society in contrast to a purely private or subjective morality (*Moralität*). For Hegel the ethical life is expressed in three arenas: family, civil society, and the state. See *Philosophy of Right*, pp. 187–380, §§142–360.

logically deduced from them. Hegel should not have concealed this, for after all he had studied the Greeks.

One not infrequently hears people who become engrossed in clichés for lack of losing themselves in studies say that a light shines over the Christian world, whereas paganism is shrouded in darkness. This sort of talk has always seemed strange to me, since every more profound thinker, every more serious artist still rejuvenates himself in the eternal youth of the Greek people. Such a statement may be explained by one not knowing what one should say but only that one should say something. It is all right to say that paganism did not have faith, but if something is supposed to have been said by that, then one must be a little clearer about what one understands by faith, since otherwise one relapses into such clichés. It is easy to explain the whole of existence, including faith, without having a conception of what faith is, and one is not the worst calculator in life who counts on being admired when one has such an explanation, for as Boileau says: "A fool always finds a greater fool who admires him."[63]

Faith is precisely this paradox, that the single individual as the particular is higher than the universal and is justified over against the latter not as subordinate but superior to it, yet in such a way, mind you, that it is the single individual who, after having been subordinate to the universal as the particular, now through the universal becomes the single individual who as the particular is superior to it; [faith is this paradox] that the single individual as the particular stands in an absolute relation to the absolute. This standpoint cannot be mediated, for all mediation occurs precisely by virtue of the universal; it is and forever remains a paradox, inaccessible to thought. And yet faith is this paradox or else (these are the consequences I would ask the reader to bear in mind[64] at every point, even though it would be too prolix for me to write them down everywhere), or else faith has never existed just because it has always existed, or else Abraham is lost.

<hr />

[63] *un sot trouve toujours un plus sot, qui l'admire.* From *L'Art poétique*, 1, 232, by Nicolas Boileau-Despréaux (1636–1711), French poet, satirist, and critic. See *Œuvres de Boileau*, I–IV, ed. Berriat Saint-Prix (Paris: C. H. Langlois: Delaunay, 1830), II, p. 190, or more recently, *Boileau Œuvres*, ed. Georges Mongrédien (Paris: Editions Garnier Frères, 1961), p. 165. In English see *Boileau: Selected Criticism*, trans. Ernest Dilworth (Indianapolis: Bobbs–Merrill, 1965), p. 17.

[64] *in mente.*

That for the single individual this paradox can easily be confused with a temptation is certainly true, but one ought not for that reason to conceal it. That many people may be wholly constituted in such a way that it repulses them is certainly true, but one ought not for that reason to make faith into something different in order to be able to have it as well, but ought rather to admit that one does not have it, while those who have faith ought to be prepared to post some criteria by which to distinguish the paradox from a temptation.

Now the story of Abraham contains such a teleological suspension of the ethical. There has been no lack of keen heads and thorough scholars who have found analogies to it. Their wisdom amounts to the pretty proposition that basically everything is the same. If one will look a little closer, I doubt very much whether one will find a single analogy in the whole world except a later one[65] that proves nothing if it is certain that Abraham represents faith and that it is properly expressed in him, whose life is not only the most paradoxical that can be thought but so paradoxical that it cannot be thought at all. Abraham acts by virtue of the absurd, for the absurd is precisely that he as the single individual is higher than the universal. This paradox cannot be mediated, for as soon as Abraham sets out to do that he must admit that he was in a state of temptation, and if that is so, he never gets to the point of sacrificing Isaac, or if he has sacrificed Isaac he must then repentantly return to the universal. He gets Isaac back again by virtue of the absurd. Abraham is therefore at no moment a tragic hero but something entirely different, either a murderer or a believer. Abraham lacks the middle term that saves the tragic hero. That is why I can understand a tragic hero but cannot understand Abraham, even though in a certain demented sense I admire him more than all others.

Abraham's relation to Isaac, ethically speaking, is quite simply this, that the father must love the son more than himself. Yet the ethical has within its own scope several gradations. We shall see whether this story contains any sort of higher expression for the ethical that can ethically explain his behavior, ethically justify him in suspending the ethical duty to the son, yet without therefore moving beyond the teleology of the ethical.

---

[65] Perhaps an allusion to Jesus Christ.

When an undertaking of concern to a whole people is impeded, when such an enterprise is brought to a standstill by heaven's disfavor, when the angry deity sends a dead calm that mocks all efforts, when the soothsayer carries out his sad task and proclaims that the deity demands a young girl as sacrifice – then the father heroically must bring this sacrifice.[66] He must conceal his pain magnanimously even though he could wish he was "the lowly man who dares to weep,"[67] not the king who must act regally. And however solitarily the pain penetrates his breast, he has only three confidants[68] among the people, and soon the whole population will be privy to his pain but also to his deed, that for the welfare of all he would sacrifice her, his daughter, the lovely young maiden. "O bosom! O fair cheeks, flaxen hair" (v. 687).[69] And the daughter will move him with her tears, and the father will avert his face, but the hero will raise the knife. – Then when the news about that reaches the ancestral home, the beautiful maidens of Greece will blush with enthusiasm, and if the daughter was to be a bride, the betrothed would not be angry but proud of participating in the father's deed, because the maiden belonged to him more tenderly than to the father.

When that brave judge[70] who saved Israel in the hour of need binds God and himself in one breath by the same vow, heroically he will transform the young girl's jubilation, the beloved daughter's joy to sorrow, and all Israel will grieve with her over her maidenly youth. But every freeborn man will understand, every stouthearted woman will admire Jephthah, and every maiden in Israel will wish to act as his daughter did, for what is the use of Jephthah having conquered by means of his vow if he did not keep it? Would not the victory be taken away again from the people?

---

[66] A reference to *Iphigenia in Aulis* by the Greek dramatist Euripides (480–406 BCE). When the Greek fleet could not sail from Aulis to conquer Troy because of a dead calm, the soothsayer Calchas urged Agamemnon, king of the Greeks and commander of the Greek forces, to sacrifice his daughter Iphigenia to the goddess Artemis in hopes of persuading her to grant them a fair wind.

[67] *Ibid.* See *The Complete Greek Tragedies*, I–IV, ed. David Grene and Richard Lattimore (Chicago: University of Chicago Press, 1992), IV, p. 316, l. 445.

[68] Calchas, Odysseus, and Menelaus (*ibid.*, p. 301, l. 105).

[69] Line reference to the Danish translation of *Iphigenia I Aulis* in Euripides, trans. Christian Wilster (Copenhagen: C. A. Reitzel, 1840). See KSKB 1115. In English, see *The Complete Greek Tragedies*, IV, 330, l. 681, p. 125: "O breast and cheeks! O golden hair!"

[70] Jephthah. See Judges 11:30–40, where Jephthah vows to sacrifice the first creature that comes out of his house (which happens to be his daughter) upon his return from defeating the Ammonites with divine help.

When a son forgets his duty,[71] when the state entrusts the father with the sword of judgment, when the laws demand punishment from the father's hand, the father heroically must forget that the guilty one is his son. He magnanimously must conceal his pain, but there will not be a single person among the people, not even the son, who will fail to admire the father. And whenever the laws of Rome are interpreted, it must be remembered that many interpreted them more learnedly but none more gloriously than Brutus.

However, if Agamemnon, while a favorable wind was carrying the fleet at full sail to its destination, had dispatched that messenger who fetched Iphigenia to be sacrificed; if Jephthah, without being bound by any vow that determined the fate of the people, had said to his daughter, "grieve now for two months over your brief youth, and then I will sacrifice you"; if Brutus had had a righteous son and yet had summoned the lictors[72] to execute him – who then would have understood them? If upon being asked why they did it these three men had answered, "it is a trial in which we are being tested," would anyone then have understood them better?

When at the decisive moment Agamemnon, Jephthah, and Brutus heroically have overcome the pain, heroically have lost the beloved and merely must complete the deed externally, there never will be a noble soul in the world without tears of sympathy for their pain and tears of admiration for their deed. However, if at the decisive moment these three men were to add to the heroic courage with which they bore their pain the little phrase, "but it will not happen," who then would understand them? If as an explanation they added, "we believe it by virtue of the absurd," who then would understand them better? For who would not easily understand that it was absurd, but who would understand that one could then believe it?

The difference between the tragic hero and Abraham is obvious. The tragic hero still remains within the ethical. He lets an expression of the ethical have its telos in a higher expression of the ethical; he reduces the ethical relation between father and son or daughter and father to a

---

[71] When the sons of Lucius Junius Brutus, consul of Rome c. 500 BCE, took part in a conspiracy to restore Tarquin the former king, Brutus had them put to death. See Livy, *The Early History of Rome*, bks. I–V of *The History of Rome from its Foundation*, trans. Aubrey de Sélincourt (Harmondsworth, UK: Penguin, 1960), bk. II, §§1–6, pp. 108–13. See also KSKB 1256: *Titi Livii Historiarum libri*, I–X, ed. C. F. Ingerslev (Copenhagen: Gyldendal, 1831), I, bk. II, §§1–6, pp. 119–29.

[72] Minor Roman officials who went before the chief magistrate in public carrying the fasces or bundle of rods wrapped around an axe as a symbol of his authority.

sentiment that has its dialectic in its relation to the idea of the ethical life. Here, then, there can be no question of a teleological suspension of the ethical itself.

The case is different with Abraham. By his act he transcended the whole of the ethical and had a higher telos outside, in relation to which he suspended it. For I would certainly like to know how Abraham's act can be brought into relation to the universal, whether any connection can be discovered between what Abraham did and the universal other than that Abraham overstepped it. It is not to save a people, not to uphold the idea of the state, not to appease angry gods that Abraham does it. If there could be any question of the deity being angry, then he still was angry only at Abraham, and Abraham's whole deed stands in no relation to the universal, it is a purely private undertaking. While the tragic hero is therefore great by his ethical virtue, Abraham is great by a purely personal virtue. There is no higher expression for the ethical in Abraham's life than this, that the father must love the son. There can be no question at all of the ethical in the sense of the ethical life. Insofar as the universal was present, it was still latent in Isaac, hidden so to speak in Isaac's loins, and must then cry out with Isaac's mouth: "Do not do it, you are destroying everything."

Why does Abraham do it then? For God's sake, and what is altogether identical with this, for his own sake. He does it for God's sake because God demands this proof of his faith; he does it for his own sake so that he can prove it. Hence the unity is quite rightly expressed in the word always used to denote this relation: it is a trial, a temptation. A temptation; but what does that mean? That which ordinarily tempts a person, to be sure, is whatever would keep him from doing his duty, but here the temptation is the ethical itself, which would keep him from doing God's will. But what then is the duty? Well, the duty is precisely the expression for God's will.

Here the necessity of a new category for understanding Abraham becomes apparent. Such a relationship to the divine is unknown in paganism. The tragic hero does not enter into any private relation to the deity, but the ethical is the divine and therefore the paradox in it can be mediated in the universal.

Abraham cannot be mediated, which can also be expressed by saying he cannot speak. As soon as I speak, I express the universal, and if I do not do that, then no one can understand me. As soon as Abraham wants to

52

express himself in the universal, he must say that his situation is a temptation, for he has no higher expression for the universal that ranks above the universal he oversteps.

While Abraham therefore arouses my admiration, he appalls me as well. Whoever denies himself and sacrifices himself for duty gives up the finite in order to grasp the infinite and is secure enough; the tragic hero gives up the certain for the even more certain, and the eye of the beholder rests confidently upon him. But the one who gives up the universal in order to grasp something still higher that is not the universal, what does he do? Is it possible that this can be anything other than a temptation? And if it is possible but the single individual then made a mistake, what salvation is there for him? He suffers all the pain of the tragic hero, he destroys his joy in the world, he renounces everything and perhaps at the same moment blocks himself from the sublime joy which was so precious to him that he would buy it at any price. The observer cannot understand him at all, nor confidently rest his eyes upon him. Perhaps what the believer intends cannot be done at all since it is indeed inconceivable. Or if it could be done but the individual has misunderstood the deity, what salvation would there be for him? The tragic hero needs and demands tears, and where was the envious eye so arid that it could not weep with Agamemnon? But where was the one whose soul was so confused that he had the audacity to weep over Abraham? The tragic hero accomplishes his deed at a definite moment of time, but in the course of time he does something no less significant; he visits someone whose soul is enveloped by sorrow, whose breast cannot get air because of its anguished sighs, whose thoughts, pregnant with tears, weigh heavy upon him. The tragic hero appears before him, breaks the spell of sorrow, loosens the corset, and elicits the tears as the sufferer forgets his sufferings in the tragic hero's. One cannot weep over Abraham. One approaches him with a religious awe,[73] as Israel approached Mount Sinai.[74] – What if, then, the lonely man who climbs Mount Moriah, which at its peak towers sky-high over the plains of Aulis, what if he is not a sleepwalker who goes safely across the precipice while the one standing at the foot of the mountain looking on trembles with anxiety and out of respect and fright does not once dare call to him – what if he becomes flustered, what if he has made a mistake! – Thanks! Again thanks be to a man who offers the one who has

---

[73] *horror religiosus.*   [74] Exodus 19:12–13.

been overcome by life's sorrows and left behind naked, offers him the expression, the leaf of the word, with which he can hide his wretchedness.[75] Thanks be to you, great Shakespeare, you who can say everything, everything, everything exactly as it is – and yet why did you never give expression to this torment? Did you perhaps reserve it for yourself, like the beloved whose name one cannot bear the world even to mention?[76] For a poet buys this power of the word to tell everybody else's dark secrets at the cost of a little secret he cannot divulge, and a poet is not an apostle, he casts out devils only by the power of the devil.[77]

But if the ethical is indeed teleologically suspended in this manner, how then does the single individual in whom it is suspended exist? He exists as the particular in contrast to the universal. Does he then sin? For this is the form of sin, viewed ideally, so that even though the child does not sin because it is not conscious of its existence as such, its existence, viewed ideally, is nevertheless still sin, and the ethical exacts its claim upon the child at every moment. If one denies that this form can be repeated in such a way that it is not sin, then judgment has fallen upon Abraham. How then did Abraham exist? He believed. That is the paradox by which he remains at the apex and which he cannot make clear to anyone else, for the paradox is that he as the single individual places himself in an absolute relation to the absolute. Is he justified? His justification is again the paradox, for if he is justified, it is not by virtue of being something universal but by virtue of being the particular.

How does the single individual assure himself that he is justified? It is easy enough to level all existence to the idea of the state or the idea of a society. If one does that, then it is also easy enough to mediate, for then one does not come at all to the paradox that the single individual as the particular is higher than the universal, which I can also express appropriately in a proposition of Pythagoras to the effect that the odd number is more perfect than the even number.[78] Insofar as one occasionally

---

[75] Cf. Genesis 3:7.

[76] See the dedication by T. T. (presumably the editor, Thomas Thorpe) that prefaced the first edition of the sonnets and *A Lover's Complaint* by the English poet and dramatist William Shakespeare (1564–1616).

[77] Cf. Mark 3:22.

[78] Kierkegaard's source for this information was Wilhelm Gottlieb Tennemann, *Geschichte der Philosophie*, I–XI (Leipzig: Bei Johann Ambrosius Barth, 1798–1819), I, pp. 105–6. See JP 5:5616 and KSKB 815–26. On the pre-Socratic philosopher Pythagoras (c. 570–497 BCE) and the later Pythagorean school of thought, see W. G. K. Guthrie, *A History of Greek Philosophy*, I–VI (Cambridge: Cambridge University Press, 1969), I, pp. 146–340.

hears a reply tending toward the paradox in our age, it generally goes like this: "One judges it according to the outcome." A hero who has become an offense or stumbling block[79] to his age in the awareness that he is a paradox that cannot make itself intelligible cries out confidently to his contemporaries: "The outcome will indeed show that I was justified." This cry is rarely heard in our age, for just as it does not produce heroes, which is its defect, so also it has the advantage of producing few caricatures. When someone in our age hears these words, "it will be judged according to the outcome," then it is clear right away with whom one has the honor of speaking. Those who talk this way are a numerous lot whom I shall designate by the common name of "associate professors." Secured in life, they live in their thoughts; they have a *permanent* position and *secure* prospects in a well-organized state; they have centuries or indeed even millennia between themselves and the earthquakes of existence; they do not fear that such things can be repeated, for what indeed would the police and newspapers say? Their task in life is to judge the great men and to judge them according to the outcome. Such conduct toward the great betrays a curious mixture of arrogance and wretchedness – arrogance because they feel called to pass judgment, wretchedness because they do not feel their lives are even remotely related to those of the great. Surely anyone with only a smattering of nobility of nature[80] has not become a completely cold and clammy worm, and when he approaches the great it can never escape his mind that since the creation of the world it has been customary for the result to come last and that if one is in truth to learn anything from the great, it is precisely the beginning to which one must be attentive. If the one who is to act wants to judge himself by the outcome, then he will never begin. Even though the outcome may delight the whole world, it cannot help the hero, for he only came to know the outcome when the whole thing was over, and he did not become a hero by that but by the fact that he began.

Moreover, the outcome (insofar as it is finitude's answer to the infinite question) is in its dialectic altogether heterogeneous to the hero's existence. Or would it be possible to prove that Abraham was justified in relating himself as the single individual to the universal by the fact that he

---

[79] σκανδαλον. Cf. 1 Corinthians 1:23.　　[80] *erectioris ingenii.*

got Isaac by a *miracle*? If Abraham actually had sacrificed Isaac, would he therefore have been less justified?

But people are curious about the outcome, just as they are about the outcome of a book. They do not want to know anything about the anxiety, the distress, the paradox. They flirt esthetically with the outcome; it comes just as unexpectedly but also just as easily as a prize in the lottery, and when they have heard the outcome they are edified. And yet no robber of churches who toils in irons is so base a criminal as the one who plunders the holy in this way, and not even Judas,[81] who sold his Lord for thirty pieces of silver, is more contemptible than the one who peddles greatness in this way.

It goes against the grain for me to speak inhumanly about the great, to let it darken into an indefinite form at a great distance, to let it be great without bringing out the human element in it, without which it ceases to be great. For it is not what happens to me that makes me great but what I do, and there is surely no one who thinks that a man became great because he won the grand prize in the lottery. Even if a person were born in humble circumstances, I would still insist that he not be so inhuman towards himself as to be unable to imagine the king's castle except at a distance, vaguely dreaming about its greatness and wanting thereby to elevate and destroy it at the same time because he elevated it in a base manner. I insist that he be human enough to step forward there with confidence and dignity as well. He must not be so inhuman as rudely to offend everyone by storming into the king's hall from off the street, thereby losing more than the king. On the contrary, he should find pleasure in observing every dictate of propriety with glad and confident enthusiasm, which is precisely what will make him frank and open. This is only a simile, for that difference is only a very imperfect expression for the distance of spirit. I insist of every person that he must not think so inhumanly of himself that he dare not enter those palaces where not only the memory of the chosen lives but where they themselves reside. He must not rudely push himself forward and impute his kinship with them. He must be happy every time he bows before them, but he must be frank and confident and always be something more than a nurses' aide, for if he does not want to be more than that, he will never be admitted there. And what will help him is precisely the anxiety and distress in which the great

---

[81] Matthew 26:15.

are tried, for otherwise, if he has a scrap of backbone they will merely arouse his righteous envy. And what can be great only at a distance, what people want to make into something great by the help of empty and hollow phrases – that they themselves destroy.

Who was ever so great in the world as that favored woman, the mother of God, the Virgin Mary?[82] And yet how does one speak of her? That she was favored among women does not make her great, and if it did not so oddly happen that those who hear can think just as inhumanly as those who speak, then every young girl must indeed ask: "Why was I not also favored?" And if I had nothing else to say, I would not at all dismiss such a question as stupid, for with respect to a favor, abstractly viewed, every person is equally entitled. One leaves out the distress, the anxiety, the paradox. My thought is as pure as anyone's, and the thought of one who can think this way will surely become pure, and if that is not so, he has something frightful to expect as well. For anyone who has once evoked these images cannot get rid of them again, and if he sins against them, then they take terrible revenge through a quiet wrath more frightful than the clamor of ten ferocious critics. Certainly Mary bore the child miraculously, but it still went with her after the manner of women,[83] and this time is one of anxiety, distress, and paradox. The angel was surely a ministering spirit, but he was not an obliging spirit who went to the other young maidens in Israel and said: "Do not despise Mary, something extraordinary is happening to her." The angel appeared only to Mary, and no one could understand her. After all, what woman was more offended against than Mary? And is it not also true here that the one whom God blesses he curses in the same breath? This is the spirit's understanding of Mary, and she is by no means – which shocks me to say but is even more shocking that people have thoughtlessly and frivolously understood her in this way – she is by no means a lady who parades in her finery and plays with a divine child. When she then nevertheless says, "behold, I am the handmaid of the Lord,"[84] she is therefore great, and I think it should not be difficult to explain why she became the mother of God. She needs no worldly admiration, just as little as Abraham needs tears, for she was no heroine and he was no hero, but they both by no means became greater than these by being exempt from distress and torment and the paradox but became that through them.

[82] Luke 1:28–38. [83] Menses. Cf. Genesis 18:11; 31:35. [84] Luke 1:38.

57

It is great when the poet in presenting his tragic hero for public admiration dares to say: "Weep for him, for he deserves it." For it is great to deserve the tears of those who deserve to shed tears; it is great that the poet dares to keep the crowd under control, dares to chastise people so that each examines himself as to whether he is worthy to weep for the hero, for the wastewater of blubberers is a debasement of the holy. – Yet greater than all this is that the knight of faith dares to say even to the noble person who wants to weep for him: "Do not weep for me, but weep for yourself."[85]

One is moved, one returns to those beautiful times when sweet, tender longings lead one to the goal of one's desire, to see Christ walking about in the promised land. One forgets the anxiety, the distress, the paradox. Was it so easy a matter not to make a mistake? Was it not appalling that this person who walked among others was God? Was it not terrifying to sit down to eat with him? Was it so easy a matter to become an apostle? But the outcome, the eighteen centuries, it helps; it lends a hand to that paltry deception whereby one deceives oneself and others. I do not feel brave enough to wish to be contemporary with such events, but for that reason I do not judge harshly of those who made a mistake nor slightly of those who saw the right thing.

But I return to Abraham. During the time before the outcome, Abraham was either at every moment a murderer or we are at the paradox that is higher than all mediations.

The story of Abraham contains, then, a teleological suspension of the ethical. As the single individual he became higher than the universal. This is the paradox that cannot be mediated. How he entered into it is just as inexplicable as how he remains in it. If that is not the case with Abraham, then he is not even a tragic hero but a murderer. To want to continue calling him the father of faith, to speak about it to people who do not concern themselves with anything but words, is thoughtless. A human being can become a tragic hero by his own strength, but not the knight of faith. When a person sets out on what in a certain sense is the hard way of the tragic hero, many will be able to advise him; the one who goes faith's narrow way, him no one can advise, no one can understand.

---

[85] Luke 23:28.

Faith is a miracle, and yet no human being is excluded from it, for that which unites all human life is passion,[a] and faith is a passion.

Problem II: Is there an absolute duty to God?[90]

The ethical is the universal and as such in turn the divine. It is therefore right to say that every duty, after all, is duty to God, but if no more can be said, then one is saying as well that I really have no duty to God. Duty becomes duty by being referred to God, but in the duty itself I do not enter into relation to God. For instance, it is a duty to love one's neighbor. It is a duty by its being referred to God, but in the duty I do not enter into a relation to God but to the neighbor I love. If I say then in this connection that it is my duty to love God, I am really only stating a tautology insofar as "God" here is understood in an entirely abstract sense as the divine, i.e. the universal, i.e. the duty. The whole existence of the human race rounds itself off in itself as a perfect sphere and the ethical is at once its limit and its completion. God becomes an invisible vanishing point, an impotent thought, his power being only in the ethical, which completes existence. Insofar as it might occur to a person to want to love God in some sense other than the one indicated here, he is being

---

[a] Lessing[86] has somewhere expressed something similar from a purely esthetic point of view. He really wants to show in the passage that sorrow also can yield a witty expression. To this end he quotes a reply on a particular occasion by the unhappy king of England, Edward II.[87] In contrast to that he quotes from Diderot[88] a story about a peasant woman and a reply of hers. Then he continues: "That too was wit and moreover the wit of a peasant woman; but the circumstances made it unavoidable. Consequently, one must not seek the justification of witty expressions of pain and sorrow in the fact that the person who said them is refined, well-bred, reasonable, and at the same time a witty person; *for the passions make everyone equal again*, but only in the sense that everyone, without exception, would say the same thing in the same circumstances. The peasant woman's thought is one a queen could and must have been able to express, just as whatever the king said on that occasion could no doubt have been said by a peasant too." See *Collected Works*, Vol. 30, Letters, p. 223.[89]

[86] Gotthold Ephraim Lessing (1729–1781), German dramatist, drama critic, and philosopher whose writings had a formative influence upon Kierkegaard.

[87] Edward II (1284–1327) was king of England from 1307 to 1327.

[88] Denis Diderot (1713–84) was a French author and encyclopedist.

[89] *Auszüge aus Lessing's Antheil an den Litteraturbriefen*, letter 81, in *Gotthold Ephraim Lessing's sämmtliche Schriften*, I–XXXII (Berlin: Nicolaischen, 1825–28), XXX, p. 223. See KSKB 1747–62.

[90] Cf. Immanuel Kant, *Religion within the Boundaries of Mere Reason*, ed. and trans. Allen Wood and George di Giovanni (Cambridge: Cambridge University Press, 1998), pp. 100, 179–80, and *The Conflict of the Faculties* in *Religion and Rational Theology*, ed. and trans. Allen Wood and George di Giovanni (Cambridge: Cambridge University Press, 1996), pp. 124, 204, 282–3, where Kant also briefly addresses this issue with respect to Abraham and the moral law.

quixotic, he loves a phantom, which if it only had enough strength to speak would say to him: "I do not ask for your love, just stay where you belong." Insofar as it might occur to a person to want to love God differently, this love would be just as suspicious as the love which Rousseau mentions whereby a person loves the Kaffirs instead of loving his neighbor.[91]

Now if what has been advanced here is true, if there is nothing incommensurable in a human life except the incommensurability that is there only by accident, from which nothing follows insofar as existence is considered ideally, then Hegel is right. But he is not right in speaking about faith or in allowing Abraham to be regarded as its father, for by the latter he has passed sentence both on Abraham and on faith. In Hegelian philosophy the outer[92] (the externalization)[93] is higher than the inner.[94] This is often illustrated by an example. The child is the inner, the man the outer; hence the child is determined precisely by the outer, and conversely the man as the outer by the inner. Faith, on the contrary, is this paradox, that inwardness is higher than outwardness, or to recall a previous expression, that the odd number is higher than the even.[95]

In the ethical view of life, then, the single individual's task is to divest himself of the qualification of inwardness and to express this in an outward form. Whenever the single individual shrinks from doing so, whenever he wants to stay within or slip down again into the inward qualification of feeling, mood, etc., he commits an offense and stands in temptation. The paradox of faith is this, that there is an inwardness that is incommensurable with the outer, an inwardness that, mind you, is not identical with that first one but is a new inwardness.[96] This must not be overlooked. Recent philosophy has presumed without further ado to substitute the immediate for "faith." If one does that, then it is ludicrous to deny that faith has existed at all times. In that way faith is put into

[91] Probably a reference to *Emile ou de l'Education*, I–IV (Paris: Duchesne, 1762–92) by the French writer and philosopher, Jean-Jacques Rousseau (1712–1778). See KSKB 939–40. However, in this work Rousseau contrasts neighbor love to love of the medieval Mongolian and Turkish tribes called Tartars or Tatars, not the Kaffirs, a South African Bantu tribe. In English see *Emile or On Education*, trans. Allan Bloom (New York: Basic Books, 1979), p. 39.

[92] *das Äussere.*   [93] *die Entäusserung.*

[94] *das Innere.* See *The Encyclopedia Logic*, 204–13, §§135–41.   [95] See Problem I, n. 78.

[96] On faith as a new or second form of inwardness or immediacy, see JP, 1:9, 49, 84, 85, 214, 235, 972, 1032; 2:1101, 1123, 1215, 1335, 1942, 1943; 3:3560, 3561; 5:6135.

rather vulgar company with feeling, mood, idiosyncrasy, hysteria,[97] etc. To this extent philosophy may be right in saying that one ought not to stop at that. But there is nothing that justifies philosophy in this usage. Faith is preceded by a movement of infinity; only then does faith commence, unexpectedly,[98] by virtue of the absurd. This I can well understand without therefore professing to have faith. If faith is nothing beyond what philosophy passes it off to be, then Socrates has already gone further, much further, instead of the converse, that he did not arrive at it. Intellectually, he has made the movement of infinity. His ignorance is the infinite resignation. This task is already adequate for human strength, even though it is disdained in our age; but only when it is done, only when the single individual has exhausted himself in the infinite, only then is the point reached where faith can break forth.

The paradox of faith then is this, that the single individual is higher than the universal, that the single individual, to recall a now rather rare theological distinction, determines his relation to the universal by his relation to the absolute, not his relation to the absolute by his relation to the universal. The paradox can also be expressed by saying that there is an absolute duty to God, for in this relationship of duty the single individual relates himself as the single individual absolutely to the absolute. When in this connection it is said that it is a duty to love God, something different from the foregoing is meant by that, for if this duty is absolute, then the ethical is reduced to the relative. It does not follow from this that the ethical should be abolished, but it receives an entirely different expression, a paradoxical expression, in such a way, for example, that love for God can cause the knight of faith to give his love for the neighbor the opposite expression of what duty is ethically speaking.

If this is not so, then faith has no place in existence; faith is thus a temptation, and Abraham is lost since he yielded to it.

This paradox cannot be mediated, for it is due precisely to the fact that the single individual is only the single individual. As soon as this single individual wants to express his absolute duty in the universal, becomes conscious of this in the latter, he perceives himself to be in a temptation and then, if he otherwise resists it, does not come to fulfill the so-called absolute duty; and if he does not resist it, then he sins, even if his act in

---

[97] *vapeurs.*   [98] *nec opinate.*

reality[99] is equivalent to that which was his absolute duty. So what should Abraham have done? If he were to say to another person, "I love Isaac more than anything in the world and that is why it is so hard for me to sacrifice him," the other person might very well have shaken his head and said, "why sacrifice him then?" Or if the other had been an astute fellow, he would probably even have seen through Abraham and perceived that he wore his heart on his sleeve in glaring contradiction to his act.

In the story of Abraham we find such a paradox. His relation to Isaac, ethically expressed, is this, that the father must love the son. This ethical relation is reduced to the relative in contradistinction to the absolute relation to God. To the question why, Abraham has no other answer than that it is a trial, a test, which, as noted above, is the unity of its being for God's sake and for his own sake. These two qualifications also correspond to one another [as opposites] in ordinary usage. Thus if one sees a person do something that does not conform to the universal, one says he hardly did it for God's sake, meaning thereby that he did it for his own sake. The paradox of faith has lost the intermediate factor, i.e. the universal. On the one hand, it is the expression for the highest egoism (doing the frightful deed for one's own sake); on the other hand, it is the expression for the most absolute devotion (doing it for God's sake). Faith itself cannot be mediated into the universal, for it is thereby annulled. Faith is this paradox, and the single individual is utterly unable to make himself intelligible to anyone. One may well imagine that the single individual can make himself intelligible to another single individual in the same situation. Such a view would be unthinkable if people in our age did not try in so many ways to sneak slyly into greatness. The one knight of faith cannot help the other at all. Either the single individual himself becomes the knight of faith by assuming the paradox or he never becomes one. Partnership in these areas is utterly unthinkable. Any more detailed explanation of what is to be understood by Isaac can be given by the single individual always only to himself. And even if one could determine ever so precisely, generally speaking, what is to be understood by Isaac (which then, incidentally, would be the most ludicrous self-contradiction – to bring the single individual, who stands precisely outside the universal, under general categories when he should act precisely as the single individual who is outside the universal), the single individual would

[99] *realiter.*

never be able to convince himself of this through others, only by himself as the single individual. Therefore, even if a person were cowardly and base enough to want to become a knight of faith on someone else's responsibility, he certainly would not become one. For only the single individual becomes that as the single individual, and this is the greatness of it, which I can certainly understand without entering therein, since I lack courage; but this is also the frightfulness of it, which I can understand even better.

As is well known, in Luke 14:26 a remarkable teaching on the absolute duty to God is recited: "If anyone comes to me and does not hate his own father and mother and wife and children and brothers and sisters, yes, even his own life, he cannot be my disciple." This is a hard saying; who can bear to listen to it?[100] For that reason it is also very seldom heard. Yet this silence is only an evasion that avails nothing. The theological student, however, learns that these words occur in the New Testament, and in one or another exegetical aid[101] he finds the explanation that "to hate"[102] in this and a couple of other passages, by weakening it,[103] means: "love less, esteem less, honor not, value as nothing."[104] The context in which these words occur, however, does not seem to corroborate this tasteful explanation. For a story is found in the following verse about how someone who wants to erect a tower first makes a rough estimate of whether he is equal to it, lest he be laughed at afterward. The close connection between this story and the cited verse seems precisely to indicate that the words should be taken as frightfully as possible in order that each person may examine himself as to whether he can erect the building.

If that pious and accommodating exegete, who by haggling in this way thinks to smuggle Christianity into the world, had succeeded in convincing a person that grammatically, linguistically, and by analogy[105] this was the meaning of that passage, then he will hopefully also succeed at the same time in convincing the same person that Christianity is one of the most pitiable things in the world. For the teaching which in one of its most lyrical outpourings, where the consciousness of its eternal validity

---

[100] Cf. John 6:60.
[101] Carolo Gottlieb Bretschneider, *Lexicon manuale graeco-latinum in libros Novi Testamenti*, 2nd edn., I–II (Leipzig: Barth, 1829), II, p. 87. See KSKB 73–4.
[102] μισειν.   [103] *per* μειωσιν.   [104] *minus diligo, posthabeo, non colo, nihili facio.*
[105] κατ' αναλογιαν.

swells most strongly in it, has nothing to say but a noisy word that means nothing but merely indicates that one should be less kind, less attentive, more indifferent. The teaching which at the moment when it seems to want to say something frightful ends by driveling instead of striking with terror – that teaching certainly is not worth the trouble of standing up for.[106]

The words are frightful, yet I certainly believe one can understand them without implying that the person who has understood them therefore has the courage to do that. Thus one ought to be honest enough to admit what they say and to acknowledge their greatness even though one lacks the courage to do that oneself. Whoever behaves like that should not exclude himself from participation in the beautiful story, for in a way it does indeed contain comfort for the one who does not have courage to begin building the tower. But he must be honest and not explain this lack of courage as humility when on the contrary it is pride, whereas the courage of faith is the only humble courage.

Now it is easy to see that if the passage is to have any meaning it must be understood literally. God is the one who demands absolute love. Now whoever, on demanding a person's love, thinks in addition that this must be proved by his becoming lukewarm to everything that was otherwise dear to him is not only an egoist but foolish as well, and whoever would demand such a love simultaneously signs his own death warrant insofar as he has his life in this coveted love. For instance, a man requires his wife to leave father and mother,[107] but if he were to regard it as a proof of her extraordinary love for him that for his sake she became a lukewarm, indifferent daughter, etc., then he is more foolish than the greatest fool. If he had any idea what love is, he would then wish to discover that as a daughter and sister she was perfect in love and see in that an assurance that his wife would love him as she does nobody else in the kingdom. Thus what would be regarded as a sign of egoism and foolishness in a person may be regarded by the help of an exegete as a worthy representation of divinity.

But how then hate them? I shall not recall here the human distinction between loving and hating, not because I have so much against it, for it is after all passionate, but because it is egoistic and inappropriate here.

---

[106] A common practice in some churches when the gospel lesson is read.
[107] Cf. Matthew 19:4–6, where it is the man who leaves father and mother to be married.

However, if I regard the task as a paradox, then I understand it, i.e. I understand it in the way one can understand a paradox. The absolute duty may then bring one to do what ethics would forbid, but it can never make the knight of faith stop loving. Abraham demonstrates this. The moment he is willing to sacrifice Isaac, the ethical expression for what he does is this: he hates Isaac. But if he really hates Isaac, he can be sure that God does not ask it of him, for Cain[108] and Abraham are not identical. He must love Isaac with all his heart; inasmuch as God demands Isaac, Abraham must love him, if possible, even more dearly, and only then can he *sacrifice* him, for it is indeed this love for Isaac which by its paradoxical opposition to his love for God makes his act a sacrifice. But the distress and anxiety in the paradox is that, humanly speaking, he is utterly unable to make himself intelligible. Only at the moment when his act is in absolute contradiction to his feeling, only then does he sacrifice Isaac, but the reality of his act is that by which he belongs to the universal, and there he is and remains a murderer.

Furthermore, the passage in Luke must be understood in such a way that one perceives that the knight of faith has no higher expression of the universal (as the ethical) at all in which he can save himself. If we thus let the church require this sacrifice from one of its members, then we have only a tragic hero. For the idea of the church is not qualitatively different from that of the state, inasmuch as the single individual can enter into it by a simple mediation. Upon entering into the paradox, the single individual does not arrive at the idea of the church; he does not leave the paradox but must find either his eternal blessedness or his perdition within it. An ecclesiastical hero expresses the universal in his deed, and no one in the church, not even his father and mother, etc. will fail to understand him. But he is not the knight of faith and also has a different response from Abraham's; he does not say that it is a trial or a test in which he is being tried.

People generally refrain from citing such passages as that one in Luke. They are apprehensive of letting people loose for fear that the worst will happen once the single individual deigns to behave as the single individual. Moreover, they think that existing as the single individual is the easiest thing of all and therefore one must just coerce people into becoming the universal. I can share neither that fear nor that opinion, and for the same reason. Whoever has learned that existing as the single

---

[108] See Genesis 4:3–16, where Cain murders his brother Abel.

65

individual is the most terrifying thing of all will not be afraid of saying that it is the greatest, but he must also say it in such a way that his words scarcely become a trap for someone gone astray but rather help that person into the universal, even if his words make a little room for greatness. Whoever dares not mention such passages dares not mention Abraham either, and the notion that existing as the single individual is easy enough contains a very dubious indirect admission with respect to oneself. For anyone who actually has self-esteem and concern for his soul is convinced that whoever lives solely under his own supervision in the world at large lives more strictly and secluded than a maiden in her boudoir. It is no doubt true that there may be those who need coercion, those who, if set at liberty, would like a wild animal give free rein to selfish desire, but one must demonstrate that one does not belong to them precisely by the fact that one knows how to speak with fear and trembling. And one must speak out of respect for the great, lest it be forgotten for fear of the harm that surely will not come if spoken in such a way that one knows it is the great and knows its terrors, without which one does not know its greatness either.

Let us then consider in a little more detail the distress and anxiety in the paradox of faith. The tragic hero resigns himself in order to express the universal; the knight of faith resigns the universal in order to become the single individual. As I said, everything depends on how one is situated. Anyone who believes that it is easy enough to be the single individual can always rest assured that he is not the knight of faith, for vagabonds and vagrant geniuses are not men of faith. On the contrary, this knight knows that it is glorious to belong to the universal. He knows that it is beautiful and beneficial to be the particular individual who translates himself into the universal, one who, so to speak, personally produces a clean-cut, elegant, and insofar as possible flawless edition of himself, readable by all. He knows it is refreshing to become intelligible to oneself in the universal in such a way that he understands the latter, and every individual who understands him in turn understands the universal through him, and both rejoice in the security of the universal. He knows it is beautiful to be born as the particular individual who has his home in the universal, his friendly abode, which immediately receives him with open arms when he wants to remain in it. But he knows as well that higher than this there winds a lonely trail, narrow and steep; he knows that it is frightful to be born solitary, outside the universal, to walk without meeting a single

66

traveler. He knows very well where he is and how he relates to people. Humanly speaking, he is mad and cannot make himself intelligible to anyone. And yet it is the mildest expression to say that he is mad. If he is not viewed in this way, then he is a hypocrite, and indeed the higher he climbs on the trail, the more appalling a hypocrite he is.

The knight of faith knows that it is inspiring to surrender oneself to the universal, that it takes courage for this, but that there is also a security in it, precisely because it is for the universal. He knows that it is glorious to be understood by every noble-minded person and in such a way that the observer himself is ennobled thereby. This he knows, and he feels as though bound; he could wish that it was this task that was assigned to him. In like manner, Abraham might now and then have wished that the task was to love Isaac as a father would and should, intelligible to all, unforgettable for all time. He could wish that the task was to sacrifice Isaac for the universal, so that he could inspire fathers to illustrious deeds – and he is almost horrified by the thought that for him such wishes only constitute temptations and must be treated as such. For he knows it is a lonely trail he treads and that he accomplishes nothing for the universal but is himself only being tried and tested. Or what did Abraham accomplish for the universal? Let me speak humanly about it, purely humanly! He takes seventy years to get a son of his old age. What others get quickly enough and enjoy for a long time takes him seventy years to get. And why? Because he is being tried and tested. Is that not madness! But Abraham believed; only Sarah vacillated and got him to take Hagar as a concubine, but that is why he also had to drive her away. He receives Isaac – then he must be tried once more. He knew that it is glorious to express the universal, glorious to live with Isaac. But that is not the task. He knew it is kingly to sacrifice such a son for the universal; he personally would have found rest in it, and everyone would have rested approvingly in his deed, just as the vowel rests in its silent consonant;[109] but that is not the task – he is being tried. That Roman general renowned by his nickname Cunctator[110] stopped the enemy by his procrastination, yet

---

[109] An allusion to certain unsounded consonants in Hebrew which, inversely to what is indicated here, are said to "rest" or remain silent in the pronunciation of the vowels associated with them. See KSKB 989: J. C. Lindberg, *Hovedreglerne af den hebraiske Grammatik*, 2nd edn. (Copenhagen: Wahl, 1835).

[110] Fabius Maximus (?–203 BCE), who was dubbed Cunctator ("Delayer") for the successful delaying tactics he employed against Hannibal in 217 BCE.

what a procrastinator Abraham is in comparison with him! But he does not save the state. This is the content of a hundred and thirty years. Who can endure it? Would not his contemporaries, if there could be talk of such, say: "There is an eternal procrastination with Abraham; finally he got a son, that took long enough, then he wants to sacrifice him – is he not mad? And he could at least explain why he wants to do it, but it is always a trial." Nor could Abraham explain further, for his life is like a book that is placed under divine injunction and is not in the public domain.[111]

This is the frightful aspect. Whoever does not see this can always be sure that he is no knight of faith, but whoever does see it will not deny that even the most tried tragic hero as it were dances along in comparison with the slow and creeping progress of the knight of faith. Having perceived this and assured himself that he does not have the courage to understand it, he then may well sense the wondrous glory that knight attains in becoming God's confidant, the Lord's friend,[112] and, to speak very humanly, in saying "You"[113] to God in heaven, whereas even the tragic hero only addresses him in the third person.

The tragic hero is soon finished and at peace; he makes the infinite movement and is now secure in the universal. The knight of faith, on the contrary, is kept sleepless, for he is constantly being tried; at every moment there is a possibility of being able to return repentantly to the universal, and this possibility can just as well be a temptation as truth. Enlightenment on that score cannot be gotten from any human being, for then he is outside the paradox.

First and foremost, then, the knight of faith has the passion to concentrate in a single moment the whole of the ethical he violates in order to give himself the assurance that he actually loves Isaac with his whole heart.[a]

---

[a] I shall once again elucidate the difference between the collisions as they are encountered by the tragic hero and the knight of faith. The tragic hero assures himself that the ethical obligation is totally present in him by transforming it into a wish. Thus Agamemnon can say: "This is my proof that I am not violating my parental duty, that my duty is my only wish." Here we thus have wish and duty corresponding to one another. The happy lot in life is one that coincides, where my wish is my duty and vice versa. The task of most people in life is precisely to remain in their duty and to transform it into their wish by their enthusiasm. The tragic hero gives up his wish in order to fulfill his duty. For the knight of faith wish and duty are also identical, but he is required to give up both. If he then wants to give up his wish in resignation, he finds no rest, for it is after all his duty. If he wants to remain in his duty and in his wish, then he does not become a knight of faith, for the absolute duty demanded precisely that he must give it up. The tragic hero acquired a higher expression of duty, but not an absolute duty.

[111] *publici juris.*   [112] James 2:23; see also Isaiah 41:8; 2 Chronicles 20:7.
[113] *Du*, second person familiar address in Danish.

If he cannot do that, then he stands in temptation. Next, he has the passion to produce the whole of this assurance in the twinkling of an eye and in such a way that it is just as valid as in the first instance. If he cannot do that, then he does not get going, for he must constantly begin afresh. The tragic hero also concentrates in one moment the ethical he has transcended teleologically, but in this respect he has a place of resort in the universal. The knight of faith has simply and solely himself, and therein lies the frightfulness. Most people live in an ethical obligation in such a way that they let each day have its cares,[114] but then they never obtain this passionate concentration, this intensive consciousness. In a certain sense the universal can assist the tragic hero in attaining this, but the knight of faith is alone in everything. The tragic hero acts and finds rest in the universal. The knight of faith is kept in constant tension. Agamemnon gives up Iphigenia and having thereby found rest in the universal now proceeds to sacrifice her. If Agamemnon has not made the movement, if at the decisive moment his soul, instead of being passionately concentrated, has been absorbed in common blather about his having several daughters and that perhaps the extraordinary[115] still could happen – then naturally he is not a hero but a charity case.[116] Abraham also has the concentration of the hero, even though in him it is far more difficult since he has no place of resort at all in the universal, but he makes one more movement by which he concentrates his soul back upon the miracle. If Abraham has not done that, then he is only an Agamemnon, provided it can otherwise be explained how being willing to sacrifice Isaac can be justified when one does not benefit the universal by it.

Whether the single individual is now actually situated in a state of temptation or is a knight of faith, only the individual himself can determine. Nevertheless it is surely possible to construct out of the paradox some distinguishing characteristic that one not in it can also understand. The true knight of faith is always absolute isolation; the counterfeit knight is sectarian. The latter is an attempt to jump off the narrow way of the paradox and become a tragic hero on the cheap. The tragic hero expresses the universal and sacrifices himself for it. Instead of that, the sectarian Master Jackel[117] has a private theater, some good friends and comrades

---

[114] Cf. Matthew 6:34.   [115] *vielleicht das Ausserordentliche.*
[116] Literally, a *Hospitalslem*, an inmate in a poorhouse or charitable institution.
[117] A comic character whose name was used to designate a popular Danish puppet show.

who represent the universal almost as well as the public witnesses in *The Golden Snuffbox*[118] represent justice. The knight of faith, however, is the paradox, he is the single individual, absolutely only the single individual without any connections and complications. This is the frightfulness that the sectarian weakling cannot endure. For instead of learning from it that he is incapable of doing the great and then simply admitting it – something I naturally cannot but approve since that is what I do myself – the poor devil thinks that by joining with some other poor devils he will be able to do it. But that will not do at all; no cheating is tolerated in the world of spirit. A dozen sectarians link arms, they know nothing at all about the lonely spiritual trials[119] that await the knight of faith and which he dares not avoid, precisely because it would be still more frightful if he presumptuously forced his way forward. The sectarians deafen each other with noise and clamor, they keep anxiety away by their screaming, and a hooting menagerie[120] such as this thinks it is storming heaven and treads the same path as the knight of faith, who in the loneliness of the universe never hears any human voice but walks alone with his frightful responsibility.

The knight of faith is assigned solely to himself; he feels the pain of not being able to make himself intelligible to others, but he feels no vain desire to instruct others. The pain is to him the assurance; vain desire he does not know, his soul is too earnest for that. The counterfeit knight easily betrays himself by his instantly acquired proficiency. He does not grasp the point of the speech at all, that insofar as another individual is to go the same way he must become the single individual in exactly the same way and does not need anyone's guidance, least of all someone who wants to be obtrusive. Here again people unable to endure the martyrdom of unintelligibility jump off the path and instead of that choose, conveniently enough, worldly admiration of their proficiency. The true knight of faith is a witness, never a teacher, and therein lies the deep humanity that is worth more than this frivolous concern for the welfare of other people that is extolled under the name of sympathy but is really nothing more than vanity. The one who wants to be only a witness admits thereby that no person, not even the lowliest, needs another person's concern or is to be debased by it so that the other may be exalted. But as he himself did not gain what he gained on

---

[118] *Gulddaasen*, a comedy by Christian Olufsen (1764–1827) published in Copenhagen in 1793.
[119] *Anfægtelser*. See "A Preliminary Outpouring from the Heart," n. 17.
[120] *Dyrehaugsselskab*, literally a group at a deer park (*dyrehave*) or preserve for wild animals.

the cheap, neither does he sell it on the cheap. He is not base enough to accept the admiration of people and in return give them his silent contempt; he knows that true greatness is equally accessible to all.

Either there is then an absolute duty to God, and if there be such a thing, it is the paradox described, that the single individual as the particular is higher than the universal and as the single individual stands in an absolute relation to the absolute – or else faith has never existed because it has always existed, or else Abraham is lost, or else one must explain the passage in Luke 14 in such a way as that tasteful exegete did, and explain the corresponding[121] and similar[122] passages in the same manner.

Problem III: Was it ethically defensible of Abraham to conceal his undertaking from Sarah, from Eliezer, from Isaac?

The ethical as such is the universal; as the universal it is in turn the disclosed. Defined immediately as a sensuous and psychical being, the single individual is the concealed. His ethical task, then, is to extricate himself from his concealment and to become disclosed in the universal. Whenever he wants to remain in concealment he commits an offense and is in a state of temptation, from which he can emerge only by disclosing himself.

Here we are again at the same point. If there is no concealment that has its rationale in the single individual as the particular being higher than the universal, then Abraham's conduct is indefensible, for he disregarded the ethical intermediary forums. If there is such a concealment, however, then we are at the paradox, which cannot be mediated because it is due precisely to the single individual as the particular being higher than the universal, but the universal is precisely the mediation [of the particular]. The Hegelian philosophy assumes no justified concealment, no justified incommensurability. It is therefore consistent in demanding disclosure, but it is befuddled in wanting to regard Abraham as the father of faith and in speaking about faith. For faith is not the first immediacy but a later one.[123] The first immediacy is the esthetic, and here the Hegelian

---

[121] See Deuteronomy 13:6–10, 33:9; Matthew 10:37, 19:29.

[122] In the fair copy of the manuscript (see SKP IV B 96, 6) Kierkegaard adds in parentheses: "e.g. I Cor. 7:11." The editors of the Danish first collected edition point out, however, that I Corinthians 7:9 more aptly qualifies as a "similar" passage.

[123] See Problem II, n. 96.

philosophy may well be right. But faith is not the esthetic or else faith has never existed because it has always existed.

The best procedure here is to consider the whole matter purely esthetically and for that purpose to embark upon an esthetic deliberation to which I shall invite the reader to devote himself completely for a moment, while I for my part shall adapt my presentation to the subject matter. The category I shall consider in a little more detail is the *interesting*,[124] a category that especially in our time, precisely because we live at a turning point,[125] has acquired great importance, for it is properly the category of the turning point. Therefore one should not, as sometimes happens after personally having been infatuated with it with all one's strength,[126] disregard the category because one has outgrown it. But neither should one be too greedy for it, for it is true that to become interesting or to have an interesting life is not a task for handicrafts but a momentous privilege, which like every privilege in the world of spirit is bought only in deep pain. Thus Socrates was the most interesting person who has lived, his life the most interesting that has been led, but this existence was allotted to him by the god, and inasmuch as he himself had to achieve it, he also was not unacquainted with trouble and pain. To take such an existence in vain is unbecoming to anyone who reflects more seriously on life, and yet examples of such endeavors are not infrequently seen in our age. Moreover, the interesting is a border category, a common boundary[127] between esthetics and ethics. To a certain extent the deliberation must constantly stray over into the domain of ethics, while in order to have significance it must seize the problem with esthetic fervor and appetite. In our age ethics rarely concerns itself with such things. The reason must be that there is no room for them in the system. Thus it could be done in monographs, and furthermore, if one does not want to be long-winded, it could be done briefly and still obtain the same result, that is, provided one has the predicate in one's power, for one or two

---

[124] The category of the interesting, associated with the eccentric and bizarre, was introduced by the German romantic writer, Friedrich Schlegel (1772–1829), in *Über das Studium der griechischen Poesie*, written in 1795 and published in 1797. See KSKB 1816–25: *Friedrich Schlegel's sämmtliche Werke*, I–X (Vienna: Jakob Mayer, 1822–5), V, pp. 5–332. In English see *On the Study of Greek Poetry*, trans. Stuart Barnet (Albany: State University of New York, 2001). The interesting came to the fore as an esthetic category in Denmark in J. L. Heiberg's review of Adam Oehlenschläger's play, *Dina*, in *Intelligensblade*, nos. 16 and 17, November 15, 1842.

[125] *in discrimine rerum.*   [126] *pro virili.*   [127] *confinium.*

predicates can reveal a whole world. Should there not be room in the system for such small words?

Aristotle says in his immortal *Poetics*: "Two parts of the plot, then, reversal and discovery, are on matters of this sort" (cf. Ch. 11).[128] Naturally only the second feature concerns me here: discovery,[129] recognition. Wherever it is possible to speak of recognition, for that very reason[130] a prior concealment is implied. Just as recognition is the resolving, relaxing element in the dramatic life, so concealment is the element of tension. What Aristotle develops earlier in the same chapter concerning the various merits of tragedy, all in proportion to how reversal[131] and discovery[132] coincide, plus what he has to say about single and double recognition, cannot be taken into account here, even though in its fervor and quiet absorption it is especially tempting to one who has long been weary of the superficial omniscience of summary writers. A more general observation may be appropriate here. In Greek tragedy concealment (and consequently recognition) is an epic remnant based upon a fate in which the dramatic action disappears and from which it has its dark, mysterious source. That is why the effect produced by a Greek tragedy is similar to the impression of a marble statue that lacks the power of the eye. Greek tragedy is blind. Therefore a certain abstraction is necessary in order to be properly affected by it. A son[133] murders his father, but only afterwards learns that it is his father. A sister[134] is about to sacrifice her brother but comes to know that at the decisive moment. This sort of tragedy can be of little interest to our *reflective* age. Modern drama has given up the idea of fate, has emancipated itself dramatically, is sighted, introspective, assimilates fate into its dramatic consciousness. Concealment and disclosure are then the hero's free act for which he is responsible.

Recognition and concealment are also an essential element in modern drama. To give examples of this would be too prolix. I am courteous enough to assume that everyone in our age, which is so esthetically

---

[128] δυο μεν ουν του μυθου μερη, περι ταυτ' εστι, περιπετεια και αναγνωρισις. See *The Complete Works of Aristotle*, I–II, ed. Jonathan Barnes (Princeton: Princeton University Press, 1984), II, p. 2324 (11, 1452b). See also KSKB 1069–73: *Aristotelis Opera Omnia: Græce*, I–V, ed. Theophilus Buhle (Biponti: Ex Typographia Societatis, 1791–1800) V: *De arte poetica*, p. 224.

[129] αναγνωρισις. [130] *eo ipso.* [131] περιπετεια. [132] αναγνωρισις.

[133] Oedipus in *Oedipus Rex* by Sophocles (c. 496–406 BCE). See *The Complete Greek Tragedies*, II, pp. 9–76.

[134] Iphigenia in *Iphigenia in Tauris* by Euripides. See *The Complete Greek Tragedies*, III, pp. 343–413.

sensual, so potent and fired up that it conceives just as easily as the partridge which, according to Aristotle,[135] has only to hear the cock's voice or its flight overhead – I assume that everyone who merely hears the word "concealment" easily will be able to shake about a dozen novels and comedies out of his sleeve. For that reason I can be brief and thus immediately suggest only a more general observation. If someone playing hide-and-seek, thereby bringing about the dramatic ferment in the piece, conceals some *nonsense*, we get a comedy; if he is related to the idea, however, then he may come close to being a tragic hero. Here is just one example of the comic. A man puts on makeup and wears a wig. The same man is eager to make a hit with the fair sex; he is confident enough of success with the help of the makeup and the wig, which make him absolutely irresistible. He catches a girl and is at his zenith. Now comes the point. If he can admit his deception, will he not lose all his power to charm? When he appears as a plain, even a bald-headed man, does he not thereby lose the beloved in turn? – Concealment is his free act, for which esthetics also makes him responsible. This branch of scholarship is no friend of bald-headed hypocrites; it abandons him to ridicule. This may be enough merely to suggest what I mean; the comic cannot be a subject of interest for this investigation.

The path I have to take is to carry concealment dialectically through esthetics and ethics, for the point is to let esthetic concealment and the paradox appear in their absolute dissimilarity.

A couple of examples. A girl is secretly in love with someone without the pair having as yet definitely confessed their love for each other. Her parents force her to marry someone else (in addition it could be filial piety that motivates her); she obeys her parents and conceals her love "so as not to make the other unhappy and no one will ever have to know what she suffers." – A young lad may get possession of the object of his longings and restless dreams by a single word. But this little word will compromise, indeed perhaps (who knows?) even ruin a whole family. He nobly decides to remain concealed: "The girl must never be told so that she perhaps may become happy by another's hand." What a pity that this couple, both of whom are concealed individually from their respective loved ones, are also

---

[135] *History of Animals*, V, 5, 541a, pp. 27–30; VI, 2, 560b, pp. 13–16. See *The Complete Works of Aristotle*, I: pp. 854–5, 882; and KSKB 1079: *Aristotelis De anima*, with commentary by Friedrich Adolph Trendelenburg (Ienae: Walzii, 1833).

concealed from each other; otherwise a remarkable higher unity could be brought about here. – Their concealment is a free act for which they are also responsible esthetically. But esthetics is a civil and sentimental discipline that knows more ways out than any pawnshop manager. What does it do then? It does everything possible for the lovers. By means of a coincidence the respective partners in the prospective marriage get a hint of the other party's magnanimous decision. An explanation is forthcoming. They get each other and also a place among real heroes, for although they have not even had time to sleep on their heroic resolution, esthetics still views it as if for many years they had courageously fought to the end for their resolve. For esthetics does not take much heed of time; whether it be jest or earnestness, time goes equally fast for it.

But ethics knows nothing either of that coincidence or that sentimentality, nor does it have so fleeting a concept of time. The matter hereby acquires a different complexion. There is no use arguing with ethics, for it has pure categories. It does not appeal to experience, which of all ridiculous things is about the most ridiculous, and far from making a man wise, if anything it makes him mad if he knows nothing higher than that. Ethics has no contingency; consequently, it does not arrive at an explanation, it does not trifle with dignities, it places a huge responsibility on the frail hero's shoulders. It denounces as presumptuous his wanting to play providence by his deed, but it also denounces wanting to do that by his suffering. It enjoins believing in actuality and having courage to contend with all the hardships of actuality rather than with those anemic sufferings assumed on one's own responsibility. It warns against trusting the clever calculations of the understanding, which are more perfidious than the oracles of ancient times. It warns against any ill-timed magnanimity; let actuality deal with it, that is the time to show courage. But then ethics itself offers all possible assistance. However, if something deeper stirred in these two, if there was earnestness to see the task, earnestness to set to work, then something will surely come of them. But ethics cannot help them; it is offended because they are keeping a secret from it, a secret they have assumed on their own responsibility.

So esthetics demanded concealment and rewarded it; ethics demanded disclosure and punished concealment.

Sometimes, however, even esthetics demands disclosure. When the hero, a prey to esthetic illusion, thinks to save another person by his silence, then esthetics demands silence and rewards it. However, when the hero has a disturbing effect on another person's life through his action, then it demands disclosure. Here I approach the tragic hero and shall consider for a moment Euripides' *Iphigenia in Aulis*. Agamemnon must sacrifice Iphigenia. Esthetics now requires silence of Agamemnon, inasmuch as it would be unworthy of the hero to seek consolation from any other person, just as out of solicitude for the women he ought to conceal it from them as long as possible. At the same time, the hero, precisely in order to be a hero, must also be tried in the frightful temptation which the tears of Clytemnestra[136] and Iphigenia will cause him. What does esthetics do? It has a way out; it has an old servant in readiness who discloses everything to Clytemnestra. Now everything is in order.

However, ethics has no coincidence and no old servant standing by. The esthetic idea contradicts itself as soon as it must be carried out in actuality. Ethics therefore demands disclosure. Not being prey to any esthetic illusion, the tragic hero demonstrates his ethical courage precisely by announcing Iphigenia's fate to her himself. If he does that, then the tragic hero is ethics' beloved son in whom it is well pleased.[137] If he keeps silent, it may be because he thinks by doing so to make it easier for others, but it may also be because he thereby makes it easier for himself. But he knows himself to be free of the latter motive. If he keeps silent, he assumes a responsibility as the single individual inasmuch as he disregards any argument that may come from outside. As the tragic hero he cannot do this, for ethics loves him precisely because he constantly expresses the universal. His heroic act requires courage, but part of this courage is that he dodges no argumentation. Now it is true that tears are a frightful argument to the person,[138] and one is no doubt touched by nothing so much as by tears. In the play Iphigenia receives permission to weep; in actuality she ought to have been allowed, like Jephthah's daughter,[139] two months to weep, not in solitude but at her father's feet, and to use all her art, "which only is tears," and to entwine herself, instead of an olive branch,[140] around his knees (cf. v. 1224).

Esthetics demanded disclosure but made do with a coincidence; ethics demanded disclosure and found its satisfaction in the tragic hero.

[136] Agamemnon's wife.   [137] Cf. Mark 1:11.   [138] *argumentum ad hominem.*   [139] Judges 11:38.
[140] Cf. *The Complete Greek Tragedies*, IV, l. 1215, p. 359. The figure of the olive branch, a sign of supplication in ancient Greece, appears in the Danish translation Kierkegaard used (l. 1225, p. 145). The English translation cited here reads instead: "My body is a suppliant's, tight clinging/To your knees."

Despite the rigor with which ethics demands disclosure, it cannot be denied that secrecy and silence actually make for greatness in a person precisely because they are qualifications of inwardness. When Amor leaves Psyche, he says to her: "You will bear a child who will be a divine infant if you keep silent but a human being if you betray the secret."[141] The tragic hero, who is the favorite of ethics, is the purely human; him I can also understand, and all his undertakings are in the open as well. If I go further, I always stumble upon the paradox, the divine and the demonic, for silence is both of these. Silence is the demon's snare, and indeed the more it is silenced, the more frightful the demon becomes; but silence is also the deity's communion with the single individual.

Before proceeding to the story of Abraham, however, I shall call forward a few poetic personages. By the power of dialectic I shall hold them on end, and as I brandish the discipline of despair over them I shall surely prevent them from standing still, so that through their anxiety they might be able to bring something or other to light.[a]

In his *Politics*[144] Aristotle tells a story about a political disturbance in Delphi that originated in a marriage affair. The bridegroom, to whom the

---

[a] These movements and positions presumably could still become a subject for esthetic treatment; however, whether faith and the whole life of faith can become so I leave undecided here. Because it is always a joy for me to thank anyone to whom I am indebted, I shall just thank Lessing for the few hints about a Christian drama that are found in his *Hamburgische Dramaturgie*.[142] However, he has fastened his eyes on the purely divine side of this life (the consummate victory) and therefore has had misgivings; perhaps he would have judged otherwise if he had been more aware of the purely human side (theology of wayfarers).[143] What he says is undeniably very brief and partly evasive, but since I am always very pleased when I can find an occasion to include Lessing, I shall bring him in at once. Lessing was not only one of Germany's most erudite minds, he not only possessed a quite rare precision in his knowledge, which enables one safely to rely on him and his personal inspections without fear of being duped by loose, undocumented quotations and half-understood phrases drawn from unreliable compendia, or of becoming disoriented by a stupid trumpeting of novelties which the ancients have propounded far better – but he also had an exceedingly uncommon gift for explaining what he himself has understood. With that he stopped; in our age people go further and explain more than they themselves have understood.

[141] The story of Amor and Psyche is told in *The Golden Ass* or *Metamorphoses* by the Roman writer, Lucius Apuleius (c. CE 125–?). See KSKB 1215: *L. Apuleii Opera omnia*, I–II, ed. G. F. Hildebrand (Leipzig: Cnoblochii, 1842), I, p. 337. In English see Apuleius, *The Golden Ass*, trans. P. G. Walsh (Oxford: Clarendon Press, 1994), p. 86.

[142] *Gotthold Ephraim Lessing's sämmtliche Schriften*, XXIV, pp. 11–25. In English see *Hamburg Dramaturgy*, trans. Helen Zimmern (New York: Dover, 1962), pp. 5–9.

[143] *Theologia viatorum*, the theology of the "church militant" or the faithful on the way to salvation, as opposed to the theology of the "church triumphant," *theologia beatorum* or theology of the blessed.

[144] *Politics*, V, 4, 1303b–1304a. See *The Complete Works of Aristotle*, II: p. 2070 and KSKB 1088: *Die Politik des Aristoteles*, I–II, tr. Christian Garve (Breslau: Wilhelm Gottlieb Korn, 1799), I, pp. 407–8.

augurs[145] predicted a misfortune that would have its genesis in his
marriage, suddenly changes his plan at the decisive moment when he
comes to fetch the bride – he will not get married. I do not need more
than this.[b] In Delphi this incident hardly came off without tears; if a poet
were to adopt it, I dare say he could safely count on sympathy. Is it not
frightful that the love so often exiled in life is now deprived of heaven's
aid as well? Is not the old saying that marriage is made in heaven put to
shame here? Ordinarily it is all the tribulations and difficulties of finitude
that, like evil spirits, want to separate the lovers, but love has heaven on
its side and therefore this holy alliance conquers all enemies. Here it is
heaven itself that separates what heaven itself after all has united.[146] Who
in fact would have suspected this? Least of all the young bride. For only a
moment ago she sat in her room in all her beauty, and the lovely maidens
had painstakingly adorned her so they could champion their handiwork
before all the world and not only have joy from it but also envy; yes, joy in
that it was impossible for them to become more envious because it was
impossible for her to be more beautiful. She sat alone in her room and was
transfigured from beauty to beauty, for all that feminine art was capable
of was used worthily to adorn the worthy one. But something was still
lacking which the young maidens had not dreamed of: a veil finer, lighter,
and yet more concealing than the one in which the young maidens had
shrouded her, a bridal gown that no young maiden knew anything about
or could assist her with; indeed, not even the bride had sense enough to
help herself. It was an invisible, friendly power that, having its pleasure
in adorning a bride, enveloped her in it without her knowledge, for she
only saw how the bridegroom passed by and went up to the temple. She
saw the door close after him, and she became even more serene and
blissful, for she knew that he now belonged to her more than ever. The
door of the temple opened, he stepped out, but she cast her maidenly eyes

---

[b] According to Aristotle, the historical catastrophe was as follows: in revenge, the [bride's] family
plants a temple vessel in among his [the bridegroom's] kitchen utensils, and he is condemned as a
temple thief. However, this is immaterial, for the question is not whether the family is clever or
stupid in taking revenge. The family gains ideal significance only insofar as it is drawn into the
dialectic of the hero. Moreover, it is fateful enough that as he wants to escape from danger by not
getting married he plunges into it, plus his life comes into contact with the divine in a double
manner, first by the augur's pronouncement, next by being condemned as a temple thief.

[145] Priests in ancient Rome who foretold future events by interpreting omens, though Kierkegaard
here applies the term to Greece.
[146] Cf. Matthew 19:6.

down and therefore did not see that his face was perplexed. But he saw that heaven was seemingly envious of the bride's loveliness and of his happiness. The door of the temple opened, the young maidens saw the bridegroom step out, but they did not see that his face was perplexed, for they were busy fetching the bride. Then she stepped forth in all her maidenly meekness and yet like a mistress surrounded by her entourage of young maidens, who curtsied to her as a young maid always curtsies to a bride. Thus she stood at the head of the beautiful band and waited – it was only a moment, for the temple was directly near by – and the bridegroom came – but he passed by her door.

But here I break off; I am not a poet and go about things only dialectically. The first thing is to point out that the hero receives that information at the decisive moment. He is thus pure and unremorseful and has not irresponsibly bound himself to the beloved. Next, he has a divine pronouncement to himself, or rather against himself; he is not ruled, then, by self-conceit like those puny lovers and paramours. Furthermore, it goes without saying that the pronouncement makes him just as unhappy as the bride, even a bit more so, since he is after all the occasion [of her unhappiness]. For it is no doubt true that the augurs only predicted a misfortune for *him*, but the question is whether this misfortune is not of such a nature that by befalling him it will at the same time affect their marital happiness. What should he do now? 1) Should he keep silent, get married, and think: "Perhaps the misfortune will not come right away, and in any case I have maintained the love and not been afraid to make myself unhappy; but I must keep silent, for otherwise even this brief moment is forfeited." This sounds plausible but is not at all, for in that case he has offended the girl. By his silence he has in a sense made the girl guilty, for if she had known about the prophecy, she certainly would never have given her consent to such an alliance. In the hour of need, then, he will have to bear not only the misfortune but also the responsibility for having kept silent and her righteous indignation at his having kept silent. 2) Should he keep silent and not get married? In that case he must enter into a hoax by means of which he destroys himself in his relation to her. Esthetics would perhaps approve of this. The catastrophe could then be fashioned in conformity with the actual event, except that at the last minute an explanation would be forthcoming, which would still be after the fact since, esthetically considered, it is necessary to let him die unless this discipline could see its way to canceling that fatal prophecy. Still, however magnanimous this behavior is, it contains an offense against the girl and the reality of her love. 3) Should he speak? Naturally we must not forget that our hero is a little too poetic for renunciation of his love to have no more significance for him than an unsuccessful business venture. If he speaks, then the whole affair becomes an unhappy love story in the same vein as Axel and Valborg.[c,147] They become a couple whom heaven itself separates. But in the present case this separation is to be conceived somewhat differently since it also results from the free act of the individuals. The great difficulty with the dialectic in this affair is namely that the misfortune must befall only him. Unlike Axel and Valborg, then, they do not have a common expression for their suffering, whereas heaven indifferently separates Axel and Valborg because they are near of kin to one another. If that were the case here, then a way out would be conceivable. For since heaven does not use any visible force to separate them but leaves it up to them, it is conceivable that they would decide jointly to defy heaven together with its misfortune.

Ethics, however, will require him to speak. His heroism consists essentially, then, in giving up the esthetic high-mindedness which

---

[c] Incidentally, at this point one could go in another direction of dialectical movements. Heaven predicts a misfortune for him from his marriage; thus he could certainly dispense with getting married but not for that reason give up the girl, only live in a romantic alliance with her, which would be more than adequate for the lovers. This surely implies an offense against the girl because he does not express the universal in his love for her. However, that would be a theme for both a poet and an ethicist who wants to champion marriage. In general, if poetry were to become aware of the religious and the inwardness of individuality, it would develop far more significant themes than those with which it presently occupies itself. Indeed, time and again one hears this story in poetry: A man is bound to a girl whom he once has loved, or perhaps never truly loved, for now he has seen another girl who is the ideal. A man makes a mistake in life; it was the right street but the wrong house, for directly across the street on the second floor lives the ideal – this is supposed to be a theme for poetry. A lover has made a mistake, he has seen the beloved by candlelight and thought she had dark hair, but lo, on closer inspection she was a blonde – but the sister, she is the ideal. This is supposed to be a theme for poetry. In my opinion, any man like that is a scamp who can be intolerable enough in life but should be instantly hissed off the stage when he wants to give himself airs in poetry. Only passion against passion produces a poetic collision, not this miscellany of minute details within the same passion. When a girl, for example in the Middle Ages, assures herself after having fallen in love that earthly love is a sin and prefers a heavenly love, here is a poetic collision, and the girl is poetic, for her life is in the idea.

[147] See the drama *Axel og Valborg* by the Danish playwright Adam Oehlenschläger, in KSKB 1601–1605: *Oehlenschlägers Tragedier*, I–X (Copenhagen: A. F. Høst, 1841–49), VI, pp. 5–108. In English see *Axel and Valborg: An Historical Tragedy in five acts*, trans. Frederick Strange Kolle (New York: Grafton Press, 1906).

certainly in this case[148] could not easily be thought to have any admixture of the vanity implicit in being concealed, since it certainly must be clear to him that he still makes the girl unhappy. The reality of this heroism, however, depends on its having had its chance and annulled it, for otherwise there would be plenty of heroes, especially in our age, which has been propelled to an unparalleled proficiency in the forgery that performs the highest by skipping what lies in between.

But why this sketch, since I still get no further than the tragic hero? Because it was after all possible that it could cast light on the paradox. Everything depends on how the hero stands in relation to the augurs' pronouncement, which in one way or another will be decisive for his life. Is this pronouncement in the public domain[149] or is it a private matter?[150] The scene is in Greece; an augur's pronouncement is intelligible to everybody. I mean not only that the single individual can understand the content lexically but can understand that an augur proclaims heaven's decision to the single individual. The augur's pronouncement, then, is not only intelligible to the hero but to everybody, and no private relation to the divine results from it. He can do what he will, what is predicted there will happen, and neither by doing something nor by leaving it undone does he come into closer relation to the divine or become an object either of its grace or of its wrath. Every individual will be able to understand the outcome just as well as the hero, and there is no secret script that is legible only to the hero. If he wants to speak, then, he can very well do so, for he can make himself intelligible. If he wants to keep silent, it is because by virtue of being the single individual he wants to be higher than the universal, wants to delude himself with all sorts of fantastic notions about how she will soon forget this sorrow, etc. However, if heaven's will had not been proclaimed to him by an augur, if it had been brought to his knowledge quite privately, if it had placed itself in an altogether private relationship to him, then we are at the paradox, if, that is, it exists (for my deliberation takes the form of a dilemma); then he could not speak even if he wanted to ever so much. He would not enjoy himself in the silence but would suffer the pain of it; yet this would be for him precisely the assurance that he was justified. His silence, then, would not be due to his wanting to place himself as the single individual in an absolute relation to the *universal* but to his having been placed as the single individual in an

---

[148] *in casu.*   [149] *publici juris.*   [150] *privatissimum.*

absolute relation to the *absolute*. From what I can figure, he would then also be able to find rest in this, whereas his magnanimous silence would always be disturbed by the requirements of the ethical. On the whole, it would be desirable if esthetics one day would attempt to begin where for so many years it has ended, with the illusion of magnanimity. Once it did this it would then work hand in hand with the religious, for this power is the only one that can rescue the esthetic from its combat with the ethical. Queen Elizabeth sacrificed her love for Essex to the state by signing his death warrant.[151] This was a heroic deed, even though a little personal pique played a hand in it because he had not sent her the ring. As is well known, he had sent it, but it was held back through the malice of a lady-in-waiting. Elizabeth received news of this, so it is said, if I am not mistaken,[152] then sat for ten days with a finger in her mouth, biting it without saying a word, and after that she died. This would be a theme for a poet who knew how to pry the mouth open; otherwise it would be useful at most to a ballet master, with whom the poet in our age too often confuses himself.

Now I shall let a sketch follow along the lines of the demonic. For that I can use the legend of *Agnes and the Merman*.[153] The merman is a seducer who shoots up from his hiding place in the abyss and in wild lust grabs and breaks the innocent flower that stood by the seashore in all its gracefulness pensively inclining its head to the sighing of the sea. This has been the drift of the poets till now. Let us make a change. The merman was a seducer. He has called to Agnes and by his smooth talk has elicited what was concealed within her. She has found in the merman what she was seeking, what she was looking for down at the bottom of the sea. Agnes is willing to follow him. The merman has put her in his arms. Agnes flings her arms around his neck. She trustingly abandons herself with her whole heart to the stronger one. He is already standing on the beach, bending out over the water to dive down with his prey. – Then Agnes looks at him once more, not timidly, not doubtingly, not proud of her good fortune, not intoxicated with desire, but absolutely believing, absolutely humble like the lowly flower she took herself to be, absolutely

---

[151] On Queen Elizabeth's relation to the Earl of Essex see Lessing, *Hamburgische Dramaturgie*, in *Lessing's sämmtliche Schriften*, XXIV, pp. 163–5; or *Hamburg Dramaturgy*, pp. 57–8.

[152] *ni fallor.*

[153] A popular legend in Danish folk songs and literature. For example, Hans Christian Andersen used it for a dramatic piece by that title. See *Agnete og havmanden: dramatisk digt* (Copenhagen: B. Luno and Schneider, 1834).

confident, she entrusts her entire destiny to him with this look. – And behold! The sea no longer roars, its wild voice becomes silent; nature's passion, which is the merman's strength, leaves him in the lurch; a dead calm comes on – and Agnes is still looking at him in this way. Then the merman collapses, he cannot withstand the power of innocence, his native element becomes unfaithful to him, he cannot seduce Agnes. He takes her home again, he explains to her that he only wanted to show her how beautiful the sea was when it is calm, and Agnes believes him. – Then he returns alone and the sea rages, but the despair in the merman rages more wildly. He can seduce Agnes, he can seduce a hundred Agneses, he can charm any girl – but Agnes has triumphed and the merman has lost her. Only as prey can she become his; he cannot faithfully belong to any girl, for he is after all only a merman. I have taken the liberty of making a little change[d] in the merman. By the way, I have also changed Agnes a little, for in the legend Agnes is not entirely without guilt, as it is altogether *nonsense* and flattery as well as an insult to the female sex to imagine a seduction in which the girl has absolutely no, no, no guilt. In the legend Agnes is, to modernize my expression a bit, a woman who craves the interesting, and anyone like that can always be sure a merman is in close proximity, for mermen discover this sort with half an eye and bear down on them like a shark after its prey. It is therefore very stupid to say, or perhaps it is a rumor a merman has let

---

[d] This legend could also be treated in another way. The merman does not want to seduce Agnes, even though he has seduced many girls previously. He is no longer a merman, or if you will, he is a wretched merman who already has long been sitting at the bottom of the sea sorrowing. Yet he knows, as indeed is learned in the legend, that he can be saved by an innocent girl's love. But he has a bad conscience with respect to young girls and dares not go near them. Then he sees Agnes. Hidden in the rushes, he has already seen her many times wandering along the beach. Her beauty, her quiet self-preoccupation attracts him to her; but his soul is filled with sadness, no wild desire stirs within it. And when the merman's sighs blend with the whispering of the rushes, she turns her ear in that direction, stands still, and becomes lost in dreaming, more delightful than any woman and surely as beautiful as an angel of deliverance, who inspires the merman with confidence. The merman takes courage, approaches Agnes, wins her love, and hopes for his deliverance. But Agnes was no quiet girl, she was very fond of the roar of the sea, and the sad sighing of the waves pleased her only because the roaring within her was then stronger. She wants to be off and away, dashing wildly out into the infinite with the merman whom she loves – so she incites the merman. She disdained his humility and now his pride awakens. And the sea roars, the waves foam, and the merman embraces Agnes and plunges into the deep with her. Never had he been so wild, never so lustful, for through this girl he had hoped for his deliverance. Before long he became tired of Agnes, but her body was never found, for she became a mermaid who tempted men with her songs.

be circulated, that so-called culture protects a girl against seduction. No, existence is more impartial and equitable; there is only one means of protection and that is innocence.

We shall now give the merman a human consciousness and let his being a merman denote a human pre-existence in whose consequences his life was ensnared. There is nothing to prevent him from becoming a hero, for the step he now takes is conciliatory. He is saved by Agnes, the seducer is crushed, he has submitted to the power of innocence, he can never seduce again. But at the same instant two forces contend for him: repentance, and Agnes and repentance. If repentance alone captures him, then he is concealed; if Agnes and repentance take him, then he is disclosed.

Now if repentance seizes the merman and he remains concealed, then he has indeed made Agnes unhappy, for Agnes loved him in all her innocence. She believed it was true that at that moment when he seemed even to her to be changed, however well he hid it, he only wanted to show her the sea's beautiful stillness. With respect to passion, however, the merman himself becomes even more unhappy, for he loved Agnes with a multiplicity of passions and had a new guilt to bear besides. The demonic element in repentance will now no doubt explain to him that this is precisely his punishment, and indeed the more it torments him the better.

If he abandons himself to this demonic element, he may then make another attempt to save Agnes, just as in a certain sense one can save a person by means of evil. He knows that Agnes loves him. If he could wrest this love from Agnes, then in a way she would be saved. But how? The merman is too sensible to reckon that a candid confession would arouse her disgust. He will then perhaps try to excite all the dark passions in her, scoff at her, mock her, hold her love up to ridicule, and if possible provoke her pride. He will spare himself no anguish, for this is the deep contradiction in the demonic, and in a certain sense there is infinitely more goodness in a demoniac than in shallow people. The more selfish Agnes is, the more easily she will be deceived (for it is only very inexperienced people who think it is easy to deceive the innocent; existence is exceedingly profound, and the easiest thing is for the clever to fool the clever), but all the more terrible the merman's sufferings will become. Indeed, the more ingeniously his deception is planned, the less Agnes modestly will hide her suffering from him; she will use every means, which will not be without effect, that is, not to move him but to torment him.

By means of the demonic the merman thus would be the single individual who as the particular was higher than the universal. The demonic has the same character as the divine in that the single individual can enter into an absolute relation to it. This is the analogy, the counterpart to that paradox of which we speak. It therefore has a certain similarity that can be misleading. For instance, the merman apparently has the proof that his silence is justified in that he suffers all his pain in it. However, there is no doubt that he can speak. He can then become a tragic hero, in my opinion a grand tragic hero, if he speaks. Perhaps few will be able to grasp what constitutes the grandeur.[e] He will then have courage to wrest from himself every self-deception about being able to make Agnes happy by his art; he will have courage, humanly speaking, to crush Agnes. Incidentally, I shall just make a psychological observation here. The more selfishly Agnes has been developed, the more glaring the self-deception will be. Indeed, it is not inconceivable that it could actually happen that a merman, humanly speaking, not only could have saved an Agnes by his demonic ingenuity but could have elicited something extraordinary out of her, for a demoniac knows how to torture powers out of even the weakest person, and in his own way he can mean well towards a person.

The merman stands at a dialectical apex. If he is rescued out of the demonic in repentance, two paths are possible. He can hold himself back and remain in concealment but not rely on his ingenuity. Then he does not come as the single individual into an absolute relation to the demonic but finds repose in the counter-paradox that the divine will save Agnes. (This is how the Middle Ages would probably make the movement, for

---

[e] Now and then esthetics treats something of the sort with its usual flattery. The merman is saved by Agnes, and the whole affair ends with a happy marriage. A happy marriage! That is easy enough. However, if ethics were to propose a toast at the wedding ceremony, then I imagine it would be another matter. Esthetics throws the cloak of love over the merman so that everything is forgotten. At the same time it is careless enough to think that things happen at a marriage as at an auction, where everything is sold in the condition in which it is found at the fall of the hammer. All esthetics cares about is that the lovers get each other; it pays no attention to the rest. If only it could see what happens afterwards; but it has no time for that and promptly goes to work full time clapping a new pair of lovers together. Esthetics is the most faithless of all branches of scholarship. Everyone who has truly loved it becomes in a certain sense unhappy, but anyone who has never loved it is and remains a dumb animal.[154]

[154] *pecus.*

according to its conception the merman obviously has reverted to the monastery.) Or he can be saved by Agnes. Now this must not be understood in such a way as to suggest that by Agnes's love he would be saved from becoming a seducer in the future (this is an esthetic rescue attempt that always evades the chief concern, namely the element of continuity in the merman's life), for in this respect he is saved; he is saved insofar as he becomes disclosed. He then marries Agnes. Nevertheless, he must have recourse to the paradox. For when the single individual by his guilt has come outside the universal, he can only return to it by virtue of having come as the single individual into an absolute relation to the absolute. Now here I shall make an observation by which I say more than is said at any point previously.[f] Sin is not the first immediacy; sin is a later immediacy. In sin the single individual is already higher, in the direction of the demonic paradox, than the universal, because it is a contradiction for the universal to want to require itself of one who lacks the necessary condition.[155] If philosophy were also to imagine, among other things, that it might just cross a person's mind to want to act according to its teaching, a curious comedy could be made out of that. An ethics that ignores sin is an altogether futile discipline, but if it asserts sin, then it is for that very reason[156] beyond itself. Philosophy teaches that the immediate should be annulled.[157] That is true enough, but what is not true is that sin, any more than faith, is the immediate as a matter of course.

As long as I move in these spheres everything goes smoothly, but what is said here in no way explains Abraham, for Abraham did not become the single individual through sin; on the contrary, he was the righteous man who is God's chosen one. The analogy to Abraham will only become apparent after the single individual is brought to a position of being able to perform the universal, and now the paradox is repeated.

The merman's movements I can therefore understand, whereas I cannot understand Abraham, for it is precisely through the paradox that the merman comes to want to realize the universal. For if he remains concealed and is initiated into all the agonies of repentance, then he becomes a

---

[f] In the preceding remarks I have deliberately avoided any reference to the question of sin and its reality. The whole work is aimed at Abraham and him I can still reach through immediate categories, that is, insofar as I can understand him. As soon as sin is introduced, ethics runs aground precisely upon repentance, for repentance is the highest ethical expression but precisely as such the deepest ethical self-contradiction.

[155] *conditio sine qua non.*   [156] *eo ipso.*   [157] *ophæves.* See Problem I, n. 59.

demoniac and as such is destroyed. If he remains concealed but does not shrewdly think that by his being tormented in the bondage of repentance he can work Agnes loose, then he no doubt finds peace but is lost to this world. If he becomes disclosed and lets himself be saved by Agnes, then he is the greatest person I can imagine, for it is only esthetics that rashly thinks to praise the power of love by letting the lost one be loved by an innocent girl and thereby saved; it is only esthetics that mistakenly perceives and believes that the girl rather than the merman is the heroic figure. The merman cannot then belong to Agnes without, after having made the infinite movement of repentance, making one more movement, the movement by virtue of the absurd. He can make the movement of repentance by his own strength, but he also uses absolutely all his strength for that and therefore cannot possibly come back and grasp actuality again by his own strength. If one lacks passion enough to make neither the one nor the other movement, if one goes through life in a careless, slipshod manner, repents a little, and thus thinks the rest will be all right, then one has once and for all renounced living in the idea and therefore can very easily attain the highest and help others attain it, i.e., beguile oneself and others with the notion that things happen in the world of spirit as in a card game where everything happens by chance. One can then amuse oneself by considering how curious it is that, precisely in an age in which everyone can achieve the highest, doubt about the immortality of the soul can be so widespread,[158] for anyone who actually has made merely the movement of infinity scarcely doubts. The conclusions of passion are the only trustworthy ones, i.e., the only convincing ones. Fortunately, existence here is more charitable and loyal than what wiseacres allege, for it excludes no human being, not even the lowest; it fools no one, for in the world of spirit only the person is fooled who fools himself. It is everybody's opinion, and insofar as I dare permit myself to pass judgment on the matter, it is also my opinion, that to enter a monastery is not the highest. But by no means do I therefore think that in our age, when no one enters the monastery, everybody is greater than the

---

[158] See, for example, Ludwig Feuerbach, *Gedanken über Tod und Unsterblichkeit* (Nürnberg: J. A. Stern, 1830). In English see *Thoughts on Death and Immortality from the Papers of a Thinker,* trans. James A Massey (Berkeley: University of California Press, 1980). See also KSKB 1574–6: Poul Martin Møller, "Tanker over Mueligheden af Beviser for Menneskets Udødelighed, med Hensyn til den nyeste derhen hørende Literatur [Thoughts on the Possibility of Proving Human Immortality, with reference to the most recent relevant Literature]," *Efterladte Skrifter,* I–III (Copenhagen: Bianco Luno, 1839–43), II, pp. 158–272. See also *Filosofiske Essays og Strøtauker,* ed. Børge Madsen (Copenhagen: Gyldendal, 1965), pp. 161–217.

deep and earnest souls who found rest in a monastery. How many in our age have passion enough to think this and then to judge themselves honestly? The very idea of taking time upon one's conscience in this way, of giving it time in its sleepless perseverance to explore every single secret thought, so that if the movement is not made every moment by virtue of what is noblest and holiest in a human being, one may with anxiety and horror discover[g] and call forth, if in no other way then through anxiety itself, the dark emotions that still lie concealed in every human life, whereas when living in community with others one so easily forgets, so easily gives it the slip, in so many ways is kept afloat, gets an opportunity to start afresh. This idea alone, understood with proper respect, I believe could chasten many an individual in our age who thinks he has already attained the highest. Yet this is of little concern in our age, which [presumably] has attained the highest, whereas in fact no age has reverted to the comic so much as it has. And it is incomprehensible that the age itself has not already by a spontaneous generation[160] given birth to its hero, the demon who ruthlessly would produce the frightful play that makes the whole age laugh and forget that it is laughing at itself. For what more is existence worth than to be laughed at when one has already attained the highest by the age of twenty? And yet what higher movement has the age discovered since the day it gave up entering the monastery? Is it not a wretched worldly wisdom, prudence, cowardice that sits in the place of honor, cravenly dupes people into thinking they have attained the highest, and slyly prevents them from even attempting lesser things? Whoever has made the monastic movement has only one movement left, the movement of the absurd. How many in our age understand what the absurd is? How many in our age live in such a way that they have renounced everything or have received everything? How many are simply so honest that they know what they can and cannot do? And is it not true that insofar as one finds such people, they are most likely to be found among the uneducated and in part among women? Just as a demoniac always discloses himself without understanding himself, the age discloses

---

[g] People do not believe this in our earnest age, and yet, remarkably enough, even in the inherently more irresponsible and less thoroughly reflective age of paganism, the two authentic representatives of the Greek view of existence, "know yourself,"[159] have hinted, each in his own way, that by concentrating upon oneself one first and foremost discovers the disposition to evil. That I am thinking of Pythagoras and Socrates hardly needs to be said.

[159] γνωθι σαυτον.   [160] *generatio æquivoca.*

its defect in a kind of clairvoyance, for over and over again it demands the comic. If this were actually what the age needed, the theatre would perhaps need a new play in which someone dying of love is made to look ludicrous. Or perhaps it would be more profitable for the age if that happened among us, if the age were to witness such an event, so that for once it could find courage to believe in the power of the spirit, courage to desist from cravenly stifling its better impulses and enviously stifling them in others – through laughter. Does the age really need a ludicrous appearance[161] of a quick wit in order to have something to laugh at? Or does it not rather need such an enthusiastic figure in order to be reminded of what was forgotten?

If one wants a plot in a similar style yet more touching because the passion of repentance was not set in motion, then for that a story from the book of Tobit could be used.[162] The young Tobias wants to marry Sarah, the daughter of Raguel and Edna. A tragic context is associated with this girl. She has been given to seven men, all of whom perished in the bridal chamber. With respect to my plot, this is a defect in the story, for a comic effect is almost unavoidable at the thought of a girl's seven futile attempts to get married, although she was quite close to it, just as close as a student who failed his theological examination seven times. In the book of Tobit the accent lies elsewhere; therefore the high number is important and in a certain sense even contributes to the tragic effect, for the magnanimity of the young Tobias is all the greater, partly because he is the only son of his parents (6:15),[163] partly because the deterrent factor is more obtrusive. Consequently this feature must go. Sarah, then, is a girl who has never been in love, who still treasures a young girl's bliss, her enormous secured mortgage in life, her "authorization for happiness"[164] – to love a man with her whole heart. And yet she is more unhappy than anyone, for she knows that the evil demon who loves her will kill the bridegroom on the wedding night. I have read about much sorrow, but I doubt whether so deep a sorrow as the one residing in this girl's life is anywhere to be found. But when the unhappiness comes from outside, consolation is still to be found. If existence did not bring a person what could have

---

[161] *Erscheinung.*   [162] Tobit 6–8 in the Old Testament Apocrypha.
[163] Tobit 6:14 in the *New English Bible with the Apocrypha.*
[164] *Vollmachtbrief zum Glücke,* from the poem "Resignation" by Friedrich von Schiller (1759–1805). See KSKB 1804–15: *Schillers sämmtliche Werke,* I–XII (Stuttgart and Tübingen: J. G. Cotta, 1838), I, p. 95. See also *Friedrich Schiller Sämtliche Werke,* I–V (Munich: Carl Hanser Verlag, 1965), I, p. 130.

made him happy, it is still a consolation that he could have received it. But the unfathomable sorrow which no time can chase away, no time can heal, is to know that nothing would help even if existence did everything! A Greek writer conceals so infinitely much in his simple naïveté when he says: "For, depend upon it, no one has escaped love or ever will escape, so long as beauty exists and eyes can see" (cf. Longus, *Pastoralia*).[165] There has been many a girl who became unhappy in love, but after all she *became* so; Sarah *was* so before she became so. It is hard not to find the person to whom one can give oneself, but it is *unspeakably* hard not to be able to give oneself. A young girl gives herself and then is said to be no longer free, but Sarah was never free and yet she had never given herself. It is hard if a girl gave herself and was defrauded, but Sarah was defrauded before she gave herself. What a world of sorrow lies in store when at last Tobias is willing to marry her! What wedding ceremonials, what preparations! No girl has been defrauded as Sarah was, for she was defrauded of the highest bliss, the absolute wealth which even the poorest girl possesses, defrauded of the secure, unbounded, free, unbridled self-loss of devotion. For the heart and liver of the fish must indeed first be smoked [as a fumigation against attacks by a demon or evil spirit] by being laid upon glowing embers.[166] And how must the mother take leave of the daughter who, just as she herself is defrauded of everything, must in turn defraud the mother of her most beautiful possession. Just read the story. Edna prepared the bridal chamber, led Sarah into it, and wept, and she received her daughter's tears. And she said to her: "My child, be cheerful! The Lord of heaven and earth give you joy for this your sorrow! Daughter, be cheerful."[167] And now at the moment of the wedding one reads, that is, if one can do it for tears: "But when they both were shut up together, Tobias rose from the bed and said: 'Get up, sister, and we shall pray that the Lord may have mercy on us'" (8:4).

If a poet read this story and were to use it, I wager a hundred to one that he would center everything on the young Tobias. The story reminds us

---

[165] πάντως γὰρ οὐδεὶς Ἔρωτα ἔφυγεν ἢ φεύξεται, μέχρι ἂν κάλλος ἦ καὶ ὀφθαλμοὶ βλέπωσιν. Longus or Longinus was a Greek fiction writer of the second century CE who wrote the pastoral romance, *Daphnis and Chloe*, from which the line quoted above was taken. See KSKB 1128: *Longi Pastoralia græce & latine*, ed. Ernest Edward Seiler (Leipzig: T. O. Weigel, 1843), p. 4. The English translation is from *Daphnis and Chloe*, trans. Ronald McCail (Oxford: Oxford University Press, 2002), p. 4.

[166] Tobit 6:1–8; 8:1–3.   [167] Cf. Tobit 7:17–18.

once again of the heroic courage of being willing to risk his life in such an obvious danger, for the morning after the wedding Raguel says to Edna: "Send one of the maids out to see whether he is alive, so that, if not, I can bury him and no one will know it" (cf. 8:13).[168] This heroic courage would have been the poet's theme. I venture to propose another. Tobias acted bravely, resolutely, and chivalrously, but any man who does not have courage for that is a milksop who knows neither what love is nor what it is to be a man nor what is worth living for. He has not even grasped the little mystery that it is better to give than to receive[169] and has no idea of the great mystery that it is far more difficult to receive than to give, that is, if one has had courage to do without and did not prove a coward in the hour of need. No, Sarah is a heroine. Her I shall approach as I have never approached any girl or felt tempted in thought to approach anyone about whom I have read. For what love of God it surely takes to be willing to let oneself be healed when one is impaired in this way from the beginning without guilt, from the beginning is a shipwrecked specimen of a human being! What ethical maturity to take upon oneself the responsibility of permitting the beloved such a daring venture! What humility before another human being! What faith in God that the next moment she would not hate the man to whom she owed everything!

Let Sarah be a man and the demonic is immediately at hand. The proud, noble nature can tolerate everything, but one thing it cannot tolerate is pity. Implied in that is a humiliation that can only be inflicted on him by a higher power, for by himself he can never become an object of pity. If he has sinned, he can bear the punishment without despairing, but without guilt to be singled out from birth as a sacrifice to pity, a sweet scent in its nostrils, that he cannot endure. Pity has a curious dialectic, at one moment requiring guilt, at the next refusing it, and therefore being predestined to pity becomes increasingly frightful the more the individual's misfortune tends towards the spiritual. But Sarah has no guilt, she is thrown out as a prey to all sufferings and in addition to this must be tormented by human pity, for even I, who surely admire her more than Tobias loved her, even I cannot mention her name without saying: "The poor girl." Let a man take Sarah's place, let him know that if he wants to

---

[168] Cf. Tobit 8:12 in *The New English Bible with the Apocrypha* and in *The New Oxford Annotated Bible with the Apocrypha/Deuteronomical Books.*

[169] Acts 20:35.

love a girl an infernal spirit will come and murder the beloved on the wedding night. Then it would be quite possible that he would choose the demonic, shut himself up in himself, and speak in the way a demonic nature speaks in secret: "Thanks, but I am no friend of ceremonies and escapades, I do not at all insist on the pleasure of love, I can indeed become a Bluebeard,[170] having my delight in seeing girls die on their wedding night." Ordinarily one gets to know very little about the demonic, even though this domain has a valid claim to be explored, especially in our age, and even though the observer, if he knows at all how to establish a little rapport with the demonic, can use almost every person at least momentarily. In this respect Shakespeare is and constantly remains a hero. That vile demoniac, the most demonic figure Shakespeare has portrayed but also portrayed matchlessly – Gloucester (later Richard the Third)[171] – what made him a demoniac? Apparently his inability to bear the pity he was at the mercy of from childhood on. His monologue in the first act of *Richard the Third* is worth more than all moral systems which have no inkling of the terrors of existence or of their explanation.

> I, that am rudely stamp'd, and want love's majesty
> To strut before a wanton ambling nymph:
> I, that am curtail'd of this fair proportion,
> Cheated of feature by dissembling Nature,
> Deform'd, unfinish'd, sent before my time
> Into this breathing world scarce half made up –
> And that so lamely and unfashionable
> That dogs bark at me as I halt by them.[172]

---

[170] A fairy tale ogre created by the French writer, Charles Perrault (1628–1703), in *Les contes de ma mère l'Oye* (1697). Kierkegaard's source was perhaps the German romantic writer, Ludvig Tieck (1773–1853). See KSKB 1848–49: *Ludwig Tieck's sämmtlige Werke*, I–II (Paris: Tétot Frères, 1837), I: "Der Blaubart," pp. 436–66. In English see *Perrault's Complete Fairy Tales*, trans. A. E. Johnson et al. (New York: Dodd and Mead, 1961), pp. 78–87. The wife in the story of Bluebeard, however, did not die on her wedding night but was threatened later when she disobeyed her husband's command not to enter a room in the castle where the remains of his previous wives were kept.

[171] Before being crowned king of England in 1483, Richard III (1452–1485) was the duke of Gloucester.

[172] *King Richard the Third*, I, I, quoted from the Arden edition by Antony Hammond (London: Methuen, 1981). Kierkegaard quotes a German translation from *Shakespeare's dramatische Werke*, I–XII, trans. August Wilhelm Schlegel and Ludwig Tieck (Berlin: G. Reimer, 1839–41), III, pp. 235–6. See KSKB 1883–8.

Natures like Gloucester's cannot be saved by mediating them into an idea of society. Ethics really only makes a fool of them, just as it would be a mockery of Sarah if it were to say to her: "Why do you not express the universal and get married?" Such natures are thoroughly in the paradox, and they are by no means less perfect than other human beings, only either lost in the demonic paradox or saved in the divine paradox. Now time in and time out people have been pleased to think that witches, goblins, trolls, etc. are freaks of nature, and it is undeniable that every person has a tendency when he sees a deformed person immediately to associate that impression with moral depravity. What an enormous injustice, inasmuch as the relation ought rather to be reversed; existence itself has perverted them, just as a stepmother makes the children perverse. The fact of originally being placed outside the universal by nature or historical circumstance is the beginning of the demonic, for which the individual, however, is not personally to blame. Thus Cumberland's Jew[173] is also a demoniac, even though he does the good. Thus too the demonic can express itself as contempt for human beings, yet a contempt, mind you, that does not make the demoniac himself act contemptuously; on the contrary, his forte is in knowing that he is better than all who judge him. – Concerning all such matters the poets should be first, if anything, to sound the alarm. God knows what books the younger would-be poets now living read! Their study probably consists in learning rhymes by heart. God knows what their significance is in existence! At this moment I do not know if they have any use other than to furnish an edifying proof of the immortality of the soul, inasmuch as one can cheerfully say to oneself about them what Baggesen says about the town's poet Kildevalle: "If he is immortal, then so are we all."[174] – What is said here with reference to Sarah, almost like poetry and thus with an imaginary basis, acquires its full significance if with a psychological interest one were to probe the meaning of the old saying: "No great genius has ever existed without a touch of

---

[173] The central character in a play by the English dramatist Richard Cumberland (1732–1811) titled *The Jew*, which was published in Danish translation in 1796 and frequently performed at the Royal Theatre in Copenhagen between 1795 and 1835. Sheva the Jew was regarded as a miser and usurer, whereas in secret he was a great benefactor to others.

[174] See Jens Baggesen (1764–1826), "Kirkegaarden i Sobradise," in *Jens Baggesens danske Værker*, I–XII, ed. by his sons and C. J. Boye (Copenhagen: Andreas Seidelin, 1827–32), I, p. 282. See KSKB 1509–20.

madness."[175] For this dementia is the genius's suffering in existence; it is the expression for, if I dare say so, the divine envy, while genius is the expression for the divine partiality. Thus from the beginning the genius is disoriented in relation to the universal and brought into relation to the paradox, whether in despair over his limitations, which in his eyes transform his omnipotence into impotence, he seeks a demonic reassurance and therefore will not admit it either before God or mortals, or whether he reassures himself religiously in love for the divine. Here lie psychological topics to which it seems to me one could gladly devote a whole life, and yet we so seldom hear a word about them. In what relation does madness stand to genius? Can the one be constructed out of the other? In what sense and to what extent is the genius master of his madness? For it goes without saying that he is master of it to a certain degree, since otherwise he would indeed really be mad. However, such observations require a high degree of ingenuity and love, for to observe the brilliant is exceedingly difficult. If one were to peruse a few authors of the greatest genius with attentiveness to this, it would perhaps be possible just once, though only with much difficulty, to discover a little.

Another incident comes to mind of an individual wanting to save the universal by his concealment and silence. For this I can use the legend of *Faust*.[176] Faust is a doubter,[h] an apostate of the spirit who goes the way of the flesh. This is the purport of the poets, and while it is repeated again

---

[h] If one does not want to use a doubter, one could choose a similar figure, for example an ironist, whose sharp eye radically has seen through the ludicrousness of existence, whose secret understanding with the forces of life ascertains what the patient wishes. He knows that he has the power of laughter; if he wants to use it, he is confident of his success, and what is more, of his happiness. He knows a single voice will raise itself to restrain him, but he knows he is stronger. He knows that men can still be made to seem serious for a moment, but he knows also that secretly they long to laugh with him. He knows that a woman can still be made to hold a fan before her eyes for a moment when he speaks, but he knows that she is laughing behind the fan. He knows that the fan is not completely opaque; he knows an invisible script can be written on it. He knows that when a woman strikes at him with the fan it is because she has understood him. He is infallibly informed about how laughter sneaks in and lives secretly in a person and once it

[175] *nullum unquam exstitit magnum ingenium sine aliqua dementia.* Cf. Seneca, *On Tranquility of Mind*, 17, 10. See KSKB 1275–9: *L. Annæi Senecae Opera omnia*, I–V (Leipzig: C. Tauchnitii, 1832), IV, p. 102. Cf. also *Seneca: Moral Essays*, I–III, trans. John W. Basore (Cambridge: Harvard University Press, 1928–1935), II, pp. 284–5: *nullum magnum ingenium sine mixtura dementiae fuit* ("no great genius has ever existed without some touch of madness"). See also JP 1:1029 (SKP IV A 148).

[176] The figure of Faust, a magician and astrologer who sold his soul to the devil in return for youth, knowledge, and pleasure, was a popular German legend deriving from the life of Dr. Johann Faust, who died c. 1541. Kierkegaard's library contained several books relating to the history of this figure. See KSKB 1405, 1443, 1460–1, 1463, 1636, 1800.

and again that every age has its Faust, one poet after the other nevertheless goes undaunted down the beaten path. Let us make a small change. Faust is the doubter par excellence,[179] but he has a sympathetic nature. Even in Goethe's interpretation of Faust[180] I miss a deeper psychological insight into doubt's secret conversations with itself. In our age, when indeed everyone has experienced doubt, no poet as yet has made any step in that direction. I even think, then, that I could readily offer them royal bonds to write on in order to jot down all the large quantity they have experienced in this regard – they would scarcely write more than what could be accommodated on the front margin.

Only when one inflects Faust into himself in this way, only then can doubt make a poetic appearance, only then does he himself also really discover in actuality all its sufferings. He knows then that it is spirit which sustains existence, but he also knows that the security and joy in which people live are not grounded in the power of spirit but are easily explicable as an unreflective happiness. As doubter, as the doubter, Faust is higher than all this, and if someone wants to deceive him by making him believe one has experienced doubt, then he easily sees through it, for whoever has made a movement in the world of spirit, consequently an infinite movement, can immediately learn through the response whether

has taken up residence sits on the watch and waits. Let us imagine such an Aristophanes,[177] such a Voltaire[178] slightly altered. For he also has a sympathetic disposition, he loves life, he loves people, and he knows that even if the condemnation of laughter perhaps will educate a redeemed young generation, a multitude of people in the present age will be ruined too. He keeps silent, then, and as far as possible even forgets to laugh. But dare he keep silent? Perhaps there are some who do not at all understand the difficulty of which I speak. They probably think that it was an admirable high-mindedness to keep silent. That is not at all what I think, for I believe that any such character, if he has not had high-mindedness in keeping silent, is a traitor against existence. Consequently, I require this high-mindedness of him. But if he has it, dare he then keep silent? Ethics is a dangerous discipline, and it was certainly possible that Aristophanes, purely for ethical reasons, decided to let laughter pass judgment on the delinquent age. Esthetic high-mindedness cannot help, for one does not venture such things on that account. If he is to keep silent, then he must enter into the paradox. – To give a hint of yet another plot, suppose, for example, a person is in possession of an explanation of a hero's life that explains it in a deplorable fashion, and yet a whole generation rests absolutely confident in this hero without suspecting anything of the sort.

[177] Aristophanes (445–388 BCE) was an Athenian writer of satirical comedies.
[178] Voltaire (1694–1778) was a French literary writer noted for his polemical, satirical, and ironic works, especially the novel *Candide* (1759).
[179] κατ' εξοχην.
[180] See *Faust I & II / Johann Wolfgang von Goethe*, ed. and trans. Stuart Atkins (Cambridge, Mass.: Suhrkamp/Insel Publishers Boston, 1984). See also KSKB 1669: Johann Wolfgang von Goethe, *Faust. Eine Tragödie*, I–II (Stuttgart and Tübingen: J. G. Cotta 1834). Goethe (1749–1832) was a celebrated German dramatist and literary critic.

it is a tried and tested man who is speaking or a Münchhausen.[181] What a Tamerlane[182] is able to do with his Huns,[183] Faust knows how to do with his doubt – to frighten people into being terror-stricken, to make the ground seem to give way under their feet, to scatter people, to cause a cry of alarm to sound everywhere. And if he does that, then he is after all no Tamerlane, he is in a certain sense warranted and has the authorization of thought. But Faust has a sympathetic nature, he loves life, his soul knows no envy, he perceives that he cannot stop the fury he no doubt can provoke, he desires no Herostratic honor.[184] – He keeps silent, he conceals the doubt more carefully in his soul than the girl who conceals the fruit of a sinful love beneath her heart, he tries as much as possible to walk in step with other people, but what goes on inside him is consumed internally, and in this way he makes himself a sacrifice to the universal.

When an eccentric pate churns up a whirlwind of doubt, one can sometimes hear people complain: "If only he had kept silent." Faust realizes this idea. Whoever has a conception of what it means to say that a person lives by spirit also knows what the hunger of doubt means and that the doubter hungers just as much for the daily bread of life as for the nourishment of the spirit. Although all the pain Faust suffers may be a very good argument for it not being pride that has possessed him, I shall still use a small measure of precaution, which is easy for me to devise, for just as Gregory of Rimini[185] was called "torturer of infants"[186] because he accepted the damnation of infants, so I could be tempted to call myself "torturer of heroes,"[187] for I am very inventive when it comes to torturing heroes. Faust sees Margaret,[188] not after having chosen lust, for my Faust does not choose lust at all. He sees Margaret, not in the concave mirror of Mephistopheles,[189] but in all her lovable innocence, and since his soul has preserved love for humankind he can very well fall in love with her. But he is a doubter; his doubt has

---

[181] A term associated with Baron Karl Friedrich Hieronymous von Münchhausen (1720–1797), a German adventurer and soldier known for his exaggerated and fanciful accounts of his exploits.

[182] Tamerlane or Timur (1336–1405) was an Asiatic conqueror renowned for his cruelty.

[183] The Huns were a savage, nomadic group of warriors led by Attila who invaded eastern and central Europe in the fourth and fifth centuries CE.

[184] The honor of destroying, after Herostratus, who burned the temple of Artemis at Ephesus in 356 BCE in order to make his name immortal.

[185] An Augustinian monk and professor at the University of Paris (d. 1358) who held that unbaptized infants went to Hell instead of Limbo as was commonly believed by Catholics at that time.

[186] *tortor infantium.*   [187] *tortor heroum.*   [188] The innocent young maid whom Faust seduces.

[189] The malevolent devil of medieval legend to whom Faust sells his soul.

destroyed actuality for him, for my Faust is so ideal that he does not belong with those scholarly doubters who doubt one hour every semester at the lectern but otherwise can do everything else, which in fact they do without the assistance of spirit or by virtue of spirit. He is a doubter, and the doubter hungers just as much for the daily bread of joy as for spiritual food. Nevertheless, he remains true to his resolve, keeps silent, and does not speak to any person of his doubt, nor to Margaret of his love.

It stands to reason that Faust is too ideal a figure to be content with the nonsense that if he spoke he would then bring about a general discussion, or that the whole affair would come off without consequence, or perhaps this, or perhaps that. (Here, as any poet will readily see, the comic element in the plot lies dormant by bringing Faust into an ironic relation to those low-comedy fools in our age who run after doubt, produce an external argument, for example a doctoral certificate, to prove they really have doubted, or swear that they have doubted everything, or prove it by the fact that on their journey they met a doubter – those couriers and sprinters in the world of spirit who in great haste get wind of doubt from one person and faith from another and now do business[190] in the best manner, according to whether the community wants to have fine sand or gravel.[191]) Faust is too ideal a figure to go about in slippers. Whoever lacks an infinite passion is not ideal, and whoever has an infinite passion has long since saved his soul from such nonsense. He keeps silent in order to sacrifice himself – or he speaks with awareness that he will put everything into disorder.

If he keeps silent, then ethics condemns him, for it says: "You must acknowledge the universal, and you acknowledge it precisely by speaking, and you dare not pity the universal." This consideration should not be forgotten when one sometimes judges a doubter severely because he speaks. I am not inclined to judge such conduct leniently, but here as everywhere it holds true that the movements must be carried out properly. If worst comes to worst, then surely a doubter, even though by speaking he brought all possible misfortune upon the world, would be far preferable to those wretched sweet-tooths who taste everything and want to cure doubt without being acquainted with it and who then as a rule are therefore the

---

[190] *wirthschafte*.

[191] A reference to the comedy *Erasmus Montanus* by Ludvig Holberg (1648–1754) in which the question is put to the people concerning the cost of burying the dead: "Do you want fine sand or common earth?" See KSKB 1566–67: *Den Danske Skue-Plads*, I–VII (Copenhagen, 1788), V, Act 1, sc. 3.

proximate cause of wild and ungovernable outbreaks of doubt. – If the doubter speaks, then he puts everything into disorder, for even if that does not happen, he only hears of it afterwards, and the outcome cannot help one either in the moment of action or with respect to responsibility.

If he keeps silent on his own responsibility, then he may well act magnanimously, but he will add a little temptation to his other pain, for the universal will constantly torment him and say: "You should have spoken. How will you find out for certain that it was not after all a hidden pride that prompted your resolve?"

However, if the doubter can become the single individual who as the particular stands in an absolute relation to the absolute, then he can receive an authorization for his silence. If so, he must turn his doubt into guilt. If so, he is in the paradox, but if so, his doubt is cured, even though he may acquire another doubt.

Even the New Testament would acknowledge such a silence.[192] Passages may even be found in the New Testament that commend irony, provided it is used to conceal something better.[193] However, this movement is just as much one of irony as any other movement that has its rationale in subjectivity being higher than actuality. People in our age do not want to know anything about this; on the whole, they do not want to know any more about irony than what has been said by Hegel,[194] who oddly enough did not understand much about it and bore a grudge against it, which our age has good reason not to give up, for it should always be on its guard against irony. The Sermon on the Mount says: "When you fast, anoint your head and wash your face, that people will not see you fasting."[195] This passage testifies directly to the fact that subjectivity is incommensurable with actuality, even that it has a right to deceive. If only the people in our age who gad about with loose talk about the idea of community[196] would read the New Testament, they might change their minds.

---

[192] See, for example, Matthew 8:4, 9:30; Mark 1:34, 44.

[193] See, for example, Matthew 21:28–32, which in the fair copy of the manuscript Kierkegaard identifies as containing "a form of irony" (JP 2:1740; SKP IV B 96:13).

[194] See *Hegel's Aesthetics*, I–II, trans. T. M. Knox (Oxford: Clarendon Press, 1975), I, pp. 64–8; *Hegel's Lectures on the History of Philosophy*, I–III, trans. E. S. Haldane (New York: Humanities Press, 1955), I, pp. 398–402; and *Philosophy of Right*, pp. 180–4, §140.

[195] Cf. Matthew 6:17–18.

[196] Probably an allusion to the Danish priest N. F. S. Grundtvig (1783–1872) and his followers, who emphasized the cultic community of the church, not the New Testament, as the foundation of Christianity.

But now Abraham, how did he act? For I have not forgotten, and the reader will now perhaps be kind enough to remember, that it was to come up against that obstacle that I embarked upon the whole preceding investigation, not so Abraham might become more intelligible by it, but so that the unintelligibility might become more conspicuous, for as was said before, I cannot understand Abraham, I can only admire him. It was also observed that none of the stages described contained an analogy to Abraham; they were only developed in order that, while being shown within their own spheres, they could indicate, so to speak, the boundary of the unknown region at the point of variation. Insofar as there could be any question of an analogy, it must be the paradox of sin, but this again lies in another sphere and cannot explain Abraham and is itself far easier to explain than Abraham.

So Abraham did not speak; he did not speak to Sarah, to Eliezer, or to Isaac. He bypassed these three ethical agents,[197] for the ethical had no higher expression than family life for Abraham.

Esthetics allowed, even demanded, silence of the single individual when he knew that by keeping silent he could save another. This already sufficiently shows that Abraham does not lie within the scope of esthetics. His silence is not at all to save Isaac, as on the whole his entire task of sacrificing Isaac for his own sake and for God's sake is an offense to esthetics, for it can well understand that I sacrifice myself, but not that I sacrifice another for my own sake. The esthetic hero was silent. Ethics convicted him, however, because he was silent by virtue of his accidental particularity. His human prescience was what determined him to be silent. This ethics cannot forgive; any human knowledge like that is only an illusion. Ethics demands an infinite movement, it demands disclosure. The esthetic hero, then, can speak but will not.

The genuine tragic hero sacrifices himself and all that is his for the universal; his deed and every emotion within him belong to the universal, he is open and in this revelation the beloved son of ethics. This does not apply to Abraham; he does nothing for the universal and is concealed.

Now we are at the paradox. Either the single individual as the particular can be in an absolute relation to the absolute, and then ethics is not the highest, or Abraham is lost; he is neither a tragic hero nor an esthetic hero.

---

[197] *Instantser*, a term associated with legal authorities and proceedings.

In a way it may seem here again that the paradox is the easiest and simplest thing of all. However, may I repeat that whoever remains convinced of this is not a knight of faith, for distress and anxiety are the only conceivable justification, even if it is not conceivable in general, for then the paradox is annulled.

Abraham keeps silent – but he *cannot* speak. Therein lies the distress and anxiety. For if I cannot make myself intelligible when I speak, I do not speak even though I go on talking incessantly day and night. This is Abraham's situation. He can say everything, but one thing he cannot say, and yet if he cannot say it, that is, say it in such a way that another person understands it, he does not speak. The relief in speaking is that it translates me into the universal. Now Abraham can say the most beautiful words any language can procure about how he loves Isaac. But this is not what at heart he has in mind to say, it is something deeper, that he is willing to sacrifice Isaac because it is a trial. No one can understand the latter, and thus everyone can only misunderstand the former. The tragic hero is unacquainted with this distress. First of all, he has the consolation that every counter-argument has had its deserts, that he has been able to give Clytemnestra, Iphigenia, Achilles,[198] the chorus,[199] every living being, every voice from the heart of humankind, every clever, every alarming, every accusing, every sympathetic thought an opportunity to stand up against him. He can be sure that everything which possibly can be said against him has been said ruthlessly, mercilessly – and to struggle against the whole world is a comfort, to struggle with oneself is frightful. He ought not to be afraid of having overlooked anything, so that one day afterwards he perhaps must cry out as King Edward IV did at the news of the murder of Clarence:[200]

> Who sued to me for him? Who, in my wrath,
> Kneel'd at my feet and bade me be advis'd?
> Who spoke of brotherhood? Who spoke of love?[i]

---

[i] Cf. Act 2, Scene 1.

[198] The young Greek hero to whom Agamemnon falsely betrothed his daughter in order to bring her to Aulis to be sacrificed to the goddess.

[199] A company of performers in Greek drama who provide an explanation and elaboration of the main action through song, dance, and narration.

[200] See Shakespeare, *King Richard the Third*, II, 1. Kierkegaard again quotes from the German translation of the text, III, p. 278, slightly changed. The king's brother George, duke of Clarence, was rashly put to death by order of the king, whose countermand arrived too late to spare him.

The tragic hero is unacquainted with the frightful responsibility of solitude. Moreover, he has the consolation that he can weep and wail with Clytemnestra and Iphigenia – and tears and cries are soothing, but unutterable sighs[201] are torturing. Agamemnon can quickly collect his soul in the certainty that he will act, and then he still has time to console and encourage. This Abraham cannot do. When his heart is stirred, when his words would contain a blessed consolation for the whole world, he dares not console, for would not Sarah, would not Eliezer, would not Isaac say to him: "Why do you want to do this then? After all, you can let it be." And if then in his distress he wanted to unburden himself and embrace all who were dear to him before proceeding to the finish, he would perhaps bring about the frightful consequence that Sarah, Eliezer, and Isaac would be offended at him and think he was a hypocrite. Speak he cannot; he speaks no human language. Even if he understood all the languages of the world, even if those loved ones also understood them, he still cannot speak – he speaks in a divine language, he speaks in tongues.[202]

This distress I can well understand. I can admire Abraham. I have no fear that anyone would be tempted by this story frivolously to want to be the single individual. But I also confess that I do not have courage for it and that I would gladly renounce any prospect of going further, if only it were possible for me to ever come that far, be it ever so late. At any moment Abraham can stop, he can repent the whole thing as a temptation; then he can speak, then everybody can understand him – but then he is no longer Abraham.

Abraham *cannot* speak, for he cannot say that which would explain everything (i.e. so it is intelligible), that it is a trial, of a sort, mind you, in which the ethical is the temptation. Anyone so situated is an emigrant from the sphere of the universal. But even less can he say the next thing. For, as was sufficiently elaborated earlier, Abraham makes two movements. He makes the infinite movement of resignation and gives up Isaac; this no one can understand because it is a private undertaking. But next, at every moment he makes the movement of faith. This is his consolation. He says, to wit: "Surely it will not happen, or if it does the Lord will give me a new Isaac, namely by virtue of the absurd." The tragic hero, however, gets to the end of the story. Iphigenia yields to her father's

---

[201] Cf. Romans 8:26. [202] Cf. 1 Corinthians 12–14.

resolve, she herself makes the infinite movement of resignation, and they now have a mutual understanding. She can understand Agamemnon because his undertaking expresses the universal. On the contrary, if Agamemnon were to say to her, "although the god demands you as a sacrifice, it is still possible that he did not demand it, that is, by virtue of the absurd," then he would at the same moment become unintelligible to Iphigenia. If he could say this by virtue of human reckoning, then Iphigenia no doubt would understand him, but then it would follow that Agamemnon had not made the infinite movement of resignation and thus would be no hero. Then the soothsayer's pronouncement is a sea captain's yarn and the whole incident is a vaudeville.

Abraham, then, did not speak. Only one word from him has been preserved, the single reply to Isaac, which also sufficiently shows that he had not spoken previously. Isaac asks Abraham where the lamb is for the burnt offering. "And Abraham said: God himself will provide the lamb for the burnt offering, my son!"[203]

This last word of Abraham I shall consider here in a little more detail. Without this word the whole incident would lack something; if it had been different, then everything would perhaps dissolve into confusion.

I have often considered to what extent a tragic hero, whether culminating in a suffering or an action, should have a final remark. In my opinion, it depends on what sphere of life he belongs to, whether his life has intellectual significance, whether his suffering or action is related to spirit.

It goes without saying that the tragic hero, like every other person who is not bereft of speech, can say a few words, perhaps a few appropriate words, at his moment of culmination, but the question is whether it is appropriate for him to say them. If the significance of his life consists in an external deed, then he has nothing to say, then everything he says is essentially chit-chat by which he only weakens the impression he makes, whereas the etiquette of tragedy enjoins him to accomplish his task silently, whether it consists in an action or in a suffering. In order not to go too far afield, I shall just take what lies closest at hand. If Agamemnon himself, not Calchas, were to have drawn the knife against Iphigenia, then he would only have demeaned himself by wanting to say a few words at the last moment, for the significance of his deed was certainly obvious to everybody. The process of piety, sympathy, feeling,

---

[203] Genesis 22:8.

and tears was complete, and his life had no relation to spirit otherwise, that is, he was not a teacher or a witness of the spirit. On the contrary, if the significance of a hero's life is oriented toward spirit, then the lack of a remark would weaken the impression he makes. What he then has to say is not a few appropriate words, a little piece of oratory, but the import of his remark is that he consummates himself at the decisive moment. An intellectual tragic hero like that should have[204] and retain the last word. He is required to have the same transfigured bearing that becomes every tragic hero, but one word is still required. If an intellectual tragic hero like that culminates in a suffering (in death), then he becomes immortal through this last word before he dies, whereas the ordinary tragic hero on the contrary only becomes immortal after his death.

Socrates[205] can be used as an example. He was an intellectual tragic hero. His death sentence is announced to him. At that moment he dies, for anyone who does not understand that the whole strength of spirit is required for dying and that the hero always dies before he dies will not get very far in his observation of life. As a hero Socrates is now required to be in a tranquil state of equilibrium, but as an intellectual tragic hero he is required to have enough spiritual strength at the final moment to fulfill himself. He cannot concentrate, then, on standing his ground over against death like the ordinary tragic hero but must make this movement so quickly that at the same moment he is consciously past this struggle and holds his own. Thus if Socrates had been silent in the crisis of death, he would then have weakened the effect of his life and aroused a suspicion that the elasticity of irony in him was not a world power but a game, the flexibility of which must be used according to an inverted scale to sustain him pathetically at the decisive moment.[j]

What is briefly suggested here is certainly not applicable to Abraham if one thinks by some analogy to be able to find an appropriate final word for

---

[j] Opinions vary about which remark of Socrates may be regarded as the decisive one, since Socrates in so many ways is poetically volatilized by Plato. I propose the following: The verdict of death is announced to him and at the same moment he dies, simultaneously overcoming death and fulfilling himself in the celebrated response that he was surprised to have been convicted by a majority of three votes.[206] No loose and idle talk in the marketplace, no foolish remark of an idiot could he have jested with more ironically than with the sentence that condemns him to death.

[204] The fair copy manuscript contains the following additional phrase at this point: "what is otherwise too often sought after in ridiculous ways."
[205] The trial of Socrates is recounted in Plato's *Apology*. See *Plato: Complete Works*, 17–36.
[206] See Plato's *Apology*, 36a. The best extant texts list the number as thirty.

Abraham. But it certainly does apply provided one perceives the necessity of Abraham having to fulfill himself at the final moment, not by silently drawing the knife but by having a word to say, since as the father of faith he has absolute significance with respect to spirit. As to what he is to say, I can form no conception in advance; after he has said it, I presumably can understand it, presumably in a certain sense can understand Abraham in what was said, yet without thereby coming any closer to him than I have previously. If no final remark by Socrates had existed,[207] then I could have imagined myself in his place and fashioned one, and had I not been able to do it, a poet would have known how, but no poet is equal to Abraham.

Before going on to consider Abraham's final word more closely, I must first point out the difficulty of Abraham coming to say anything at all. As elaborated above, the distress and anxiety in the paradox are due precisely to the silence: Abraham cannot speak.[k] In a way, then, it is a self-contradiction to demand that he should speak unless one would have him outside the paradox again, so that at the decisive moment he suspends it, whereby he then ceases to be Abraham and annuls all that preceded. Thus, if Abraham now at the decisive moment were to say to Isaac, "it is you to whom it applies," this would only be a weakness. For if he could speak at all, then he ought to have spoken long before, and the weakness would then consist in the fact that he had not had the spiritual maturity and concentration to imagine all of the pain beforehand but had shoved some aside in such a way that the actual pain was more than the imagined one. Moreover, he would fall out of the paradox by such talk, and if he really wanted to speak to Isaac, he must transform his situation into a temptation, for otherwise he could surely say nothing, and if he does that, then he is not even a tragic hero.

However, a final word by Abraham has in fact been preserved, and insofar as I can understand the paradox I can also understand Abraham's total presence in that word. First and foremost, he does not say anything, and in this form he says what he has to say. His reply to Isaac has the form

---

[k] Insofar as there can be talk of any analogy, the death scene of Pythagoras provides one such, for at his last moment he had to carry through the silence he had always maintained, and therefore he said: "It is better to be killed than to speak." Cf. Diogenes, Book 8, §39.[208]

[207] For the last words of Socrates, see Plato's *Phaedo*, which recounts the scene of his death.

[208] *Lives of the Philosophers* by Diogenes Laertius, a Greek biographer of the 3rd century CE. See KSKB 1110–11: *Diogen Laërtes Filosofiske historie*, I–II, trans. Børge Riisbrigh (Copenhagen: Andreas Seidelin, 1812), I, p. 379. In English see *Lives of the Philosophers*, trans. A. Robert Caponigri (Lanham, Md.: Regnery Publishing, 1969), p. 41.

of irony, for it is always irony when I say something and yet do not say anything. Isaac asks Abraham in the supposition that Abraham knows. Now if Abraham had replied, "I know nothing," he would have uttered an untruth. He cannot say anything, for what he knows he cannot say. He replies then: "God himself will provide the lamb for the burnt offering, my son!" From this one sees the double movement in Abraham's soul as previously described. If Abraham had merely resigned Isaac and done no more, then he would have uttered an untruth, for he indeed knows that God demands Isaac for a sacrifice, and he knows that he himself precisely at this moment is ready to sacrifice him. After having made this movement, he has at every moment made the next one, has made the movement of faith by virtue of the absurd. In principle, he utters no untruth, for by virtue of the absurd it is indeed possible that God could do something entirely different. He utters no untruth, then, but neither does he say anything, for he speaks in a foreign tongue. This becomes even more evident when we consider that it was Abraham himself who must sacrifice Isaac. Had the task been different, had the Lord commanded Abraham to bring Isaac up on Mount Moriah so he himself could let his lightning strike Isaac and take him as a sacrifice in that way, then in a literal sense Abraham would have been right in speaking as enigmatically as he does, for then he himself would not have known what would happen. But given the way the task is placed on Abraham, he himself indeed must act; so at the decisive moment he must know what he himself will do, and consequently he must know that Isaac is to be sacrificed. If he has not known this for certain, then he has not made the infinite movement of resignation. Then his words are certainly not untrue, but he is still very far from being Abraham, he is more insignificant than a tragic hero; indeed, he is an irresolute man who cannot make up his mind one way or the other and for that reason always speaks in riddles. But a vacillator like that is just a parody of the knight of faith.

Here again, then, it appears that one may well understand Abraham, but only in the way one understands the paradox. For my part, I can perhaps understand Abraham but realize as well that I do not have courage to speak in this way, no more than I have courage to act like Abraham; but by no means do I therefore say that it is something insignificant when on the contrary it is the only miracle.

And now, what did the contemporary age think of the tragic hero? That he was great and it admired him. And that honorable assembly of nobles, the jury, which every generation establishes to judge the previous generation, it judged likewise. But there was no one who could understand Abraham. And yet what did he achieve? He remained true to his love. But whoever loves God needs no tears, no admiration; he forgets the suffering in the love. Indeed, so completely has he forgotten it that there would not be the slightest trace of his pain afterwards if God himself did not remember it; for he sees in secret[209] and knows the distress and counts the tears and forgets nothing.

Either there is then a paradox, that the single individual as the particular stands in an absolute relation to the absolute, or Abraham is lost.

---

[209] Matthew 6:4; 6:18.

Epilogue

On one occasion when the price of spices in Holland became somewhat slack, the merchants let a few loads be dumped at sea in order to drive up the price. This was a pardonable, perhaps a necessary stratagem. Do we need something similar in the world of spirit? Are we so sure of having attained the highest that there is nothing left to do except piously to delude ourselves that we have not come so far in order still to have something with which to fill the time? Does the present generation need such a self-deception? Should a virtuosity in this be cultivated in it, or is it not rather sufficiently perfected in the art of self-deception? Or is what it needs not rather an honest earnestness that fearlessly and incorruptibly calls attention to the tasks, an honest earnestness that lovingly preserves the tasks, that does not make people anxiously want to rush precipitously to the highest but keeps the tasks young, beautiful, delightful to look upon, and inviting to all, yet also difficult and inspiring for the noble-minded (for the noble nature is inspired only by the difficult)? Whatever one generation learns from another, no generation learns the genuinely human from a previous one. In this respect, every generation begins primitively, has no other task than each previous generation, and advances no further, provided the previous generation has not betrayed the task and deceived itself. This genuinely human quality is passion, in which the one generation perfectly understands the other and understands itself as well. Thus no generation has learned how to love from another, no generation gets to begin at any other point than at the beginning, no later generation has a shorter task than the previous one, and if someone here is unwilling to abide with love like those previous generations but wants to go further, then that is only foolish and idle talk.

But the highest passion in a human being is faith, and here no generation begins at any other point than the previous one, every generation begins from the beginning, and the following generation goes no further than the previous one, provided the latter remained true to its task and did not leave it in the lurch. That this must be tiring is naturally something the generation cannot say, for the generation after all has the task and has nothing to do with the fact that the previous generation had the same task, unless the particular generation, or the individuals in it, presumptuously wants to occupy the place that belongs only to the spirit who governs the world and has the patience not to become tired. If the generation begins that sort of thing, it is perverse, and what wonder then that the whole of existence seems perverse to it, for there is surely no one who has found existence to be more perverse than the tailor who, according to the fairy tale, went up to heaven during his lifetime and viewed the world from that standpoint.[1] As long as the generation is concerned only with its task, which is the highest, then it cannot become tired, for the task is always sufficient for a lifetime. When the children on a holiday have already finished playing all the games before noon and now impatiently say, "is there no one who can think of a new game?," does this show then that these children are more developed and precocious than the children in the same or a previous generation who could make the familiar games last for the whole day? Or does it not rather show that these first children lack what I would call the endearing earnestness that belongs to play?

Faith is the highest passion in a human being. There are perhaps many in every generation who do not even come to it, but nobody goes further. Whether there are also many in our age who do not discover it, I do not decide; I dare only refer to myself, who does not conceal that it may not happen for a long time to come for him, yet without his therefore wishing to deceive himself or the great by making it into a trifling matter, into a childhood malady one must wish to get over as soon as possible. But life has tasks enough also for the one who does not one day come to faith, and if he honestly loves them, then his life will not be wasted, even if it never becomes like those who were sensible of and grasped the highest. But the

---

[1] "The Tailor in Heaven" from *Grimms' Fairy Tales.* See KSKB 1425–7: *Kinder- und Haus-Märchen gesammelt durch die Brüder Grimm,* 2nd edn., I–III, (Berlin: Bei G. Reimer, 1819–22), I, pp. 177–9. In English see *The Complete Fairy Tales of the Brothers Grimm,* trans. Jack Zipes (New York: Bantam Books, 1987), pp. 132–4.

one who has come to faith (whether he is extraordinarily gifted or simple-minded does not matter) does not come to a standstill in faith. Indeed, he would be shocked if someone said this to him, just as the lover would feel indignant if one said he had come to a standstill in love, for he would answer, "I am not standing still at all since I have my life in it." Yet he gets no further, nor to something else, for if he discovers the latter, then he has another explanation.

"One must go further; one must go further." This urge to go further is ancient in the world. Heraclitus the obscure,[2] who deposited his thoughts in writings and his writings in the temple of Diana[3] (for his thoughts had been his armor in life and therefore he hung it in the temple of the goddess), Heraclitus the obscure has said: "One cannot pass through the same river twice."[a] Heraclitus the obscure had a disciple who did not stop there; he went further and added: "One cannot do it even once."[b] Poor Heraclitus, to have such a disciple! By this improvement the Heraclitean thesis was amended to an Eleatic[6] thesis that denies motion, and yet that disciple only wanted to be a disciple of Heraclitus who went further, not back, to what Heraclitus had abandoned.

---

[a] "[L]ikening the things that are to the flowing of a river, he says that 'you cannot step into the same river twice.'" Cf. Plato's *Cratylus*, §402. Ast., III, p. 158.[4]
[b] Cf. Tennemann, *Gesch. d. Philos.*, I, p. 220.[5]

[2] Heraclitus (c. 540–480 BCE) was a Greek philosopher who was nicknamed "the obscure" for his cryptic method of presenting his thoughts in writing.
[3] The Roman goddess corresponding to the Greek goddess Artemis.
[4] και ποταμου ροη απειχαζων τα οντα λεγει ως δις ες τον αυτον ποταμον ουχ [αν] εμβαιης. Plato, *Cratylus*, 402a. See KSKB 1144–54: *Platonis quae exstant opera*, I–XI, ed. Fridericus Astius (Leipzig: Libraria Weidmannia, 1819–32), III, p. 158. In English see *Plato: Complete Works*, p. 120.
[5] See KSKB 815–26: W. G. Tennemann, *Geschichte der Philosophie*, I, p. 220.
[6] The Greek school of philosophy at Elea on the west coast of Italy was founded by Parmenides (c. 515–450 BCE).

Index

Cambridge texts in the history of philosophy

Titles published in the series thus far

Aquinas *Disputed Questions on the Virtues* (edited by E. M. Atkins and Thomas Williams)

Aquinas *Summa Theologiae, Questions on God* (edited by Brian Davies and Brian Leftow)

Aristotle *Nicomachean Ethics* (edited by Roger Crisp)

Arnauld and Nicole *Logic or the Art of Thinking* (edited by Jill Vance Buroker)

Augustine *On the Trinity* (edited by Gareth Matthews)

Bacon *The New Organon* (edited by Lisa Jardine and Michael Silverthorne)

Boyle *A Free Enquiry into the Vulgarly Received Notion of Nature* (edited by Edward B. Davis and Michael Hunter)

Bruno *Cause, Principle and Unity* and *Essays on Magic* (edited by Richard Blackwell and Robert de Lucca with an introduction by Alfonso Ingegno)

Cavendish *Observations upon Experimental Philosophy* (edited by Eileen O'Neill)

Cicero *On Moral Ends* (edited by Julia Annas, translated by Raphael Woolf)

Clarke *A Demonstration of the Being and Attributes of God and Other Writings* (edited by Ezio Vailati)

Classic and Romantic German Aesthetics (edited by J. M. Bernstein)

Condillac *Essay on the Origin of Human Knowledge* (edited by Hans Aarsleff)

Conway *The Principles of the Most Ancient and Modern Philosophy* (edited by Allison P. Coudert and Taylor Corse)

Cudworth *A Treatise Concerning Eternal and Immutable Morality* with *A Treatise of Freewill* (edited by Sarah Hutton)

Descartes *Meditations on First Philosophy*, with selections from the *Objections and Replies* (edited by John Cottingham)

Descartes *The World and Other Writings* (edited by Stephen Gaukroger)

Fichte *Foundations of Natural Right* (edited by Frederick Neuhouser, translated by Michael Baur)

Fichte *The System of Ethics* (edited by Daniel Breazeale and Günter Zöller)

Herder *Philosophical Writings* (edited by Michael Forster)

Hobbes and Bramhall on Liberty and Necessity (edited by Vere Chappell)

Humboldt *On Language* (edited by Michael Losonsky, translated by Peter Heath)

Kant *Anthropology from a Pragmatic Point of View* (edited by Robert B. Louden with an introduction by Manfred Kuehn)

Kant *Critique of Practical Reason* (edited by Mary Gregor with an introduction by Andrews Reath)

Kant *Groundwork of the Metaphysics of Morals* (edited by Mary Gregor with an introduction by Christine M. Korsgaard)

Kant *Metaphysical Foundations of Natural Science* (edited by Michael Friedman)

Kant *The Metaphysics of Morals* (edited by Mary Gregor with an introduction by Roger Sullivan)

Kant *Prolegomena to any Future Metaphysics* (edited by Gary Hatfield)

Kant *Religion within the Boundaries of Mere Reason and Other Writings* (edited by Allen Wood and George di Giovanni with an introduction by Robert Merrihew Adams)

Kierkegaard *Fear and Trembling* (edited by C. Stephen Evans and Sylvia Walsh)

La Mettrie *Machine Man and Other Writings* (edited by Ann Thomson)

Leibniz *New Essays on Human Understanding* (edited by Peter Remnant and Jonathan Bennett)

Lessing *Philosophical and Theological Writings* (edited by H. B. Nisbet)

Malebranche *Dialogues on Metaphysics and on Religion* (edited by Nicholas Jolley and David Scott)

Malebranche *The Search after Truth* (edited by Thomas M. Lennon and Paul J. Olscamp)

Medieval Islamic Philosophical Writings (edited by Muhammad Ali Khalidi)

Melanchthon *Orations on Philosophy and Education* (edited by Sachiko Kusukawa, translated by Christine Salazar)

Mendelssohn *Philosophical Writings* (edited by Daniel O. Dahlstrom)

Newton *Philosophical Writings* (edited by Andrew Janiak)

Nietzsche *The Antichrist, Ecce Homo, Twilight of the Idols and Other Writings* (edited by Aaron Ridley and Judith Norman)

Nietzsche *Beyond Good and Evil* (edited by Rolf-Peter Horstmann and Judith Norman)

Nietzsche *The Birth of Tragedy and Other Writings* (edited by Raymond Geuss and Ronald Speirs)

Nietzsche *Daybreak* (edited by Maudemarie Clark and Brian Leiter, translated by R. J. Hollingdale)

Nietzsche *The Gay Science* (edited by Bernard Williams, translated by Josefine Nauckhoff)

Nietzsche *Human, All Too Human* (translated by R. J. Hollingdale with an introduction by Richard Schacht)

Nietzsche *Thus Spoke Zarathustra* (edited by Adrian Del Caro and Robert B. Pippin)

Nietzsche *Untimely Meditations* (edited by Daniel Breazeale, translated by R. J. Hollingdale)

Nietzsche *Writings from the Late Notebooks* (edited by Rüdiger Bittner, translated by Kate Sturge)

Novalis *Fichte Studies* (edited by Jane Kneller)

Reinhold *Letters on the Kantian Philosophy* (edited by Karl Ameriks, translated by James Hebbeler)

Schleiermacher *Hermeneutics and Criticism* (edited by Andrew Bowie)

Schleiermacher *Lectures on Philosophical Ethics* (edited by Robert Louden, translated by Louise Adey Huish)

Schleiermacher *On Religion: Speeches to its Cultured Despisers* (edited by Richard Crouter)

Schopenhauer *Prize Essay on the Freedom of the Will* (edited by Günter Zöller)

Sextus Empiricus *Against the Logicians* (edited by Richard Bett)

Sextus Empiricus *Outlines of Scepticism* (edited by Julia Annas and Jonathan Barnes)

Shaftesbury *Characteristics of Men, Manners, Opinions, Times* (edited by Lawrence Klein)

Adam Smith *The Theory of Moral Sentiments* (edited by Knud Haakonssen)

Voltaire *Treatise on Tolerance and Other Writings* (edited by Simon Harvey)